'Echoes' of
Robert E. Lee High School

ECHO
/ek'-oh/

Of echoes, let two things be said. Denotatively, an echo is the replication of sound resulting from the reflection of its waves back to its source from off an obstructing surface. Connotatively, an echo is more, as poets remind us from time to time:

*"Like her ordinary cry,
Like—but oh, how different!"*
— WILLIAM WORDSWORTH

*"Our echoes roll from soul to soul,
And grow for ever and for ever."*
— ALFRED, LORD TENNYSON

"The best of a book is not the thought which it contains, but the thought which it suggests; just as the charm of music dwells not in the tones but in the echoes of our hearts."
— JOHN GREENLEAF WHITTIER

'ECHOES' OF ROBERT E. LEE HIGH SCHOOL

The First Decade, 1955–65

CLINTON CARTER, KERRY PALMER,
ROGER STIFFLEMIRE, AND JIM VICKREY

EDITORIAL COMMITTEE

JIM VICKREY, GENERAL EDITOR

FOREWORD BY RHETA GRIMSLEY JOHNSON

NEWSOUTH BOOKS
Montgomery

NewSouth Books
105 S. Court Street
Montgomery, AL 36104

Copyright © 2015 by Clinton Carter, Kerry Palmer, Roger Stifflemire, and Jim Vickrey, editors. All rights reserved under International and Pan-American Copyright Conventions. Published in the United States by NewSouth Books, a division of NewSouth, Inc., Montgomery, Alabama.

Publisher's Cataloging-in-Publication data

'Echoes' of Robert E. Lee High School : the first decade, 1955–65 /
Clinton Carter, Kerry Palmer, Roger Stifflemire, and Jim Vickrey, editors ;
with a foreword by Rheta Grimsley Johnson.
p. cm.
Includes index.

ISBN 978-1-60306-379-1 (paperback)
ISBN 978-1-60306-380-7 (ebook)

1. Education—Alabama. I. Title.

2015946195

Printed in the United States of America

IN MEMORY OF

TIMOTHY C. CARLTON

As Lee's first and longest serving principal, Mr. Carlton's leadership made the school what it had become by the early sixties—one of the outstanding public high schools in Alabama, a beacon of educational excellence and athletic achievement that illuminated a path others followed during the next half-century.

IN APPRECIATION OF
RICHARD JORDAN, '58

Principal T. C. Carlton had myriad positive effects on the lives of many of those who entered the Ann Street portals of the school. One was Richard Jordan, once a troubled member of one of the earliest Lee senior classes, now, a successful lawyer. He credits Mr. Carlton with setting him on the road to personal and professional success. It was in honor of the one man who had such a large impact on his life that Jordan committed the funds for the publication of this book.

Contents

Foreword . . . . Rheta Grimsley Johnson   ix
On Some Remembered Sights, Smells, and Sounds of Lee High School

Preface . . . . Jim Vickrey   xii

Part One—"Recalling 'Echoes' of Lee High School's Past, Still Reverberating from the First Decade"

1 The Vision . . . . Clinton Carter   3
   A New Beginning in Secondary Education in East Montgomery

2 The First Principal . . . . Clinton Carter   9
   The Man and the Vision Meet in Timothy C. Carlton

3 'Red & White' or 'Blue & Gray' . . . . Clinton Carter   18
   A New Beginning and New Traditions

4 Life at Lee in the Early Years . . . . Clinton Carter   25
   How the School Was Organized and Run
   A Fast First Year

5 Flashing Forward in Five-Year Increments . . . . Clinton Carter, Roger Stifflemire, Willie Riggins Jr., Annie Joyce (Riggins) Williams, Julia Sanders   38
   Dedication of the Lee Statue, 1960
   Robert E. Lee, the Man, the General, the Educator
   Determination to Integrate without Major Incident, 1964–65
   My Lee Experience

Part Two—"Recognizing 'Echoes' of the First Decade's Signal Accomplishments of Lee High School's Past"

6 Stars Fell on Lee High School . . . . Clinton Carter, Peter Howard   62
   The First Faculty and Staff
   Curriculum, Faculty, and Academic Atmosphere in the First Decade

7	The Quality of the Total Program .... KERRY PALMER, CLINTON CARTER, TOM HAMMETT, ROBIN BOZEMAN HARDWICH, DEBBIE KNIGHT HOOKS	77

    As Revealed in Academic and Student Activities of the Time
    The Robert E. Lee High School Band, 1955–65
    The Band Takes a Northern Tour
    Thoughts on Ellyn G. Dudley and the Choral Department
    Student Activities: "May I Have your Attention Please?"

8	Athletics: 'A Pattern for Greatness' .... ED JONES	124
9	The Quality of Education .... JIM VICKREY	162

    As Reflected Later in the Lives of Two Dozen
    Hall of Fame Members from the First Decade

PART THREE—"RECONSTRUCTING LEE HIGH SCHOOL'S POSSIBLE FUTURES IN THE DECADE AHEAD IN HARMONY WITH THE 'ECHOES' OF THE PAST"

10	'Echoes' of a Thousand Voices .... JIM VICKREY	176
11	A New Vision and Beginning .... JIM VICKREY	184

Appendices	191

    A: *A Note of Special Recognition of Mr. Richard Jordan*
    B: *1955–65 Graduates, Faculty/Staff, and Others Inducted*
        into the Robert E. Lee High School Hall of Fame
    C: *Alumni Activities*

Contributors	200
Index..	202

Foreword

On Some Remembered Sights, Smells, and Sounds of Lee High School

By Rheta Grimsley Johnson

Lee High smelled good. I realize that's not at the tiptop of anyone's requirements for academic excellence, but smell is the most evocative of all the senses. Smells produce memories. And memories are what we're dealing with here, memories of the precious variety.

The hallowed halls of Lee smelled like yeast rolls and real chalk, maybe a trace of Pine Sol and cigarette smoke wafting from restrooms. Lee was a feast for all the senses when I think back about it.

As you entered through the main door you could hear Tom Borden's band members tooting and trilling and running scales to prepare for another stellar halftime show. Not far away, Ellyn Dudley's choral room might be alive with unauthorized use of the piano, a rousing and impromptu rendition of the fight song gaining momentum until Miss Dudley walked in and all nonsense stopped. The official fight song, the one Miss Dudley insisted we learn, was not "Dixie," by the way, but rather "Hail to Ol' Lee High."

I can see the gym dressed for a pep rally, all done up in crepe paper finery, the cheerleaders wearing their demure skirts and sweater vests, leading us in a big "V-I" as Coach Chafin made his way to the podium. He was both macho and dignified. We revered him.

I can squint and imagine the comfortable darkness of the auditorium prepared for assembly, the Generals Three harmonizing on "I'll Be Seeing You" in a golden pool of spotlight. The first time I saw Terrell Finney in a play behind those scarlet curtains I knew the stage was his destiny. The first time I stood at the lectern I knew it wasn't mine.

My Lee High had a strong democracy and a middle class. That's another thing I dearly loved about it. Sure, you had your popular kids, the aforementioned cheerleaders and the hotshot football stars, the Beaus and Beauties and the deities of the homecoming court. At the opposite pole, you had a few zombies who were marking time, no list of clubs by their name in the *Scabbard*, no agonizing for them over what to wear to the prom.

Most of us, however, fell somewhere in between, not so smart as John T. Killian, not as beautiful as Lauryn Brassell, middle class but upwardly mobile, trying to be our best to be our best. We aspired to be top dog in some area or another.

When I was invited to join Leader's Club my senior year, I eagerly allowed myself to be doused in catsup at the YMCA spend-the-night initiation and wore hideous clothes, pigtails and painted-on freckles to school for an entire week. Now that was the path to true leadership.

Come to think of it, I also wore a toga made of bed sheets during Latin Week and hideous polyester pants suits and scrape-the-dirt maxi dresses during ordinary weeks. Sartorial splendor was not my thing.

Yet I had a place at Lee, a comfortable place, sure as the great general out front had his. I belonged. And there's no better feeling. For one thing, I excelled at joining clubs. At my mother's bidding, my father laid down the law one night and made me quit three extra-curricular activities. It had gotten out of hand.

Stars and Bars newspaper sponsor Wynona Hall will tell you I wasn't exactly chained to the typewriter turning out brilliant prose in her class. I mostly spent that period ostensibly trying to sell ads – and drinking milkshakes with the rest of the newspaper staff at the nearby McDonald's. I didn't write the best poems in Helen Blackshear's literary club called Scribblettes, either, though I loved the atmosphere of that writer's clique, as close to bohemian as was to be found at Lee during the 1960s. I adored singing with Miss Dudley's Choralees, though my alto was shaky. And the French Club planted seeds of desire that exhaust my budget still.

James Bozeman and Fred Guy taxed the undimpled side of my brain with their isosceles triangles and algebraic equations. Sarah Sutliff made me diagram sentences until I understood the underpinnings of literature. I learned so much at Lee. And, yet, the most important things weren't necessarily how to decline a noun or dissect a frog. The most important lessons I came away with were about people.

We lost a classmate, Donna Horne, to cancer. For many of us it was the first such loss, disabusing us of our own immortality.

My first African American teacher was Frank Johnson for biology, whose knowledge and teaching skills put a lie to most everything I'd been told about the races. He only smiled his warm smile at my arrogance and ignorance, probably realizing the bunk I'd heard all my life.

And the black classmates who joined us en masse my junior year—not only physically, but emotionally, leaving their own traditions and schools behind—were an unforgettable example of graciousness and compromise. Soon they were simply "classmates," not "black classmates," football stars and lab partners and friends.

At Lee I learned people are people, perhaps different in disposition and ambition and looks, grains of sand on a beach, yet with the same brains and hearts and imaginations and potential. It was the single most important thing I've learned in this life. Human beings with their frailties and strengths and dreams are all the same.

And for that I can say—or sing if you dare me—"Hail to Ol' Lee High."

Preface

By Jim Vickrey

The title of this little book about the first ten years of Lee High School fittingly derives from an event at the midpoint of that decade, specifically the annual Baccalaureate Service in honor of the Senior Class of 1960. I remember the service as though it had just occurred because the Baccalaureate Sermon delivered that afternoon was the most dynamic and impactful I had heard up to that time, and it remains one of the most effective sermons I have heard. It was delivered by Dr. Joel McDavid, then the senior pastor of the First United Methodist Church of Montgomery, later a bishop.

The sermon was about a real place I have never visited. Dr. McDavid used it as a metaphor for life and taught us a lesson that was perfect for the occasion. He set forth his argument: a mountain-nestled lake in Franconia Notch on the New England Coast of North America is known as Echo Lake. It not only resounds with the songs sung or words whispered or shouted into it, reporting unerringly what has been directed its way, but it also increases the volume and often enhances the quality of the sounds it receives. Echo Lake, Dr. McDavid stated, "seems to be a symbol of the moral world and the universe in which we live." Whatever we say, sing, and shout or whisper into it, we receive back in kind but with even greater volume and in the key we first directed its way. Thus, "we get out of life about as much as we put into it," except that it redounds to us enlarged in scope. That lesson of life's dividend is a parable "we can live by for the rest of our lives," he concluded.

To me, then and now, that not only was good preacherly counsel, it also was a metaphor of my own and my classmates' years at Lee High School. Lee left me then and still does with "echoes" of the enlarged returns I enjoyed whenever I sent forth melodic, positive words and songs. It also reminds me of what happens to the disharmonies I have sent forth when they are returned to me enlarged, angry, and negative.

Thus, from the beginning its editors and writers have thought of this little book of big memories and lessons of life as a compendium of as many of the strong, positive echoes as we can still discern and the few negative ones we cannot forget, for they still seem to be informing and inspiring the lives of Lee's approximately 25,000 graduates.

That explains, if not justifies, the "echoes" of the title. But the echoes which make up the principal content of the book emerged from numerous exchanges of ideas and information among the authors/editors and from the suggestions of others, and they fall roughly into three categories, delineated here as three **R**s: "**R**ecalling 'Echoes' of Lee High School's Past, Still Reverberating from the First Decade," "**R**ecognizing 'Echoes' of the First Decade's Signal Accomplishments of Lee High School's Past," and "**R**econstructing Lee High School's Possible Futures in the Decade ahead in Harmony with the 'Echoes' of the Past." Each category focuses on specific topics we hope other Lee graduates and friends will find as interesting and/or important as we did.

MOST OF THE TOPICS in the first category were researched and written by CLINTON CARTER (HOF '95), who was assistant principal of Lee High 1962–65 and later became the school's second principal and still later served as superintendent of the Montgomery County Public School System. Much of what he crafted has never been widely circulated but offers unique insights into Lee High School's earliest years, including the vision of its founders and its beginning; the leadership of founding principal Timothy C. Carlton; the new traditions occasioned by the opening of the first public high school in east Montgomery; the activities and happenings characterizing Lee's first year of 1955–56; and, flashing forward in five-year increments, the dedication of the Lee statue in the spring of 1960 and the determination to peacefully desegregate in 1964–65. With respect to the Lee statue dedication, we have also included a profile by ROGER STIFFLEMIRE ('60, HOF 2005) of Robert E. Lee, the man and educator for whom our school is named.

The second content category focuses on Lee High people and programs, particularly the successful academic, athletic, and extracurricular activities characterizing the frenzy of activity that was the Ann Street campus during its first ten years. CLINTON CARTER describes Lee's first faculty, staff, and academic program. I recognize a representative sample of HOF members from the persons so far chosen from classes making up the first generation of Lee students. KERRY PALMER ('90, HOF 2014), a protégé of Lee's first and greatest band director, Johnny Long, offers a definitive short history of the band and choral musical programs in Lee's first years. ROBIN BOZEMAN HARDWICH ('67; HOF 2009) and DEBBIE KNIGHT HOOKS ('71; HOF 2014) interestingly describe the many activities that occupied the extra-curricular time of Lee students during the late fifties and early sixties. ED JONES ('56; HOF 2010), a quarterback on Lee's first football team, brings together information on the remarkable success of Lee High's earliest athletes in football, basketball, baseball, and track and field.

The third division of the book, which I ('60, HOF '94) have mostly written, after a walk down memory lane praising its *pasts*, focuses on the possible *futures* of our Alma Mater in the Montgomery public school system, which currently faces more than its share of challenges—demographic, financial, facility-related, political, programmatic, and more. Lee High School faces similar challenges. In particular, because of impending changes to Ann Street, which fronts the length of the property on the west, decisions must be made in the near future about the present physical plant and the recommendation, still on the books of the Board of Education, to make the next new east Montgomery high school "the new Lee," as consultants from out-of-state and a citizens facilities committee advising the Board recommended several years ago. As an educator, I understand how complicated resolving such matters can be, but they must be addressed and resolved—indecision can be devastating in the public sector, where the very futures of our children and so our community are being determined.

THUS THIS BOOK IS an anthology written primarily by persons who have supplemented their unique personal experiences at Lee High School with research on the same.

The audience for *Echoes* is, of course, all past Lee High alumni, faculty, and staff and all present and prospective Lee students, faculty, and staff, along with any who support or have supported them and/or the school, and any others with sufficient connections to Lee or Lee people to enjoy reading others' recollections of their time there, and with sufficient understanding and moral sensitivity to appreciate it and to act on the basis of a call to action to preserve the values for which it stands. The book might also be useful to anyone with a general interest in public secondary education in Montgomery County.

In compiling this record of the first decade of the now six-decade history of Robert E. Lee High School, the editors and authors hope that they have selected areas of interest to all 25,000-plus graduates. Completing it, one thing is clear to me: Greek general and statesman Pericles was right to remark in his famous "Funeral Oration" how hard it is "to say neither too little nor too much when belief in the truth is hard to confirm." It *is* difficult, but we have done our best to be faithful to the facts and to avoid mere legend about Lee's people and events. We think it is better to say too little or too much rather than nothing at all.

'Echoes' of
Robert E. Lee High School

Montgomery's new Robert E. Lee High School, 1955.

1

The Vision

A New Beginning in Secondary Education in East Montgomery

By Clinton Carter

The impetus to construct Robert E. Lee High School arose from crowded conditions at Sidney Lanier High School—Montgomery's existing high school for white students—and the need to accommodate the children of increasing numbers of personnel assigned to Maxwell and Gunter Air Force bases.

The first reference to Lee High in the official minutes of the Montgomery County Board of Education is recorded on August 8, 1952. As was the custom during those years, much unofficial discussion doubtless took place between Superintendent Dr. Clarence M. Dannelly, board members, and others both before and after the August 8 meeting. Board member Gus Dozier, a resident of east Montgomery, was a key advocate for a new high school in the area; four of his children subsequently became Lee graduates.

The Board approved a 20-classroom unit with combination gym/auditorium, allocating $426,280 for construction, of which $240,000 would come from federal impact aid funds (a significant source intended to help local school systems provide for influxes of military dependents in areas with large bases).

On September 22, 1952, the City of Montgomery agreed to reimburse the Board for purchase of property on which to build the school. The agreement contains a reversionary clause in which the City would reclaim the property if it were no longer used for education.

On December 12, 1952, the Board approved necessary condemnations to clear the preferred site in the Frazierville neighborhood. Some $1,755 was paid for property belonging to Hairston (no first names were used), $1,070 to Brown, and $7,512 to Smith. The total cost of the original 12-acre site was $74,000.

Two months later, on February 13, 1953, the Board increased the size of the project to 21 classrooms plus 3 labs.

Bids were let for the initial construction on June 9, 1953. Bear Brothers Construction Company was the low bidder at $492,500. At this same meeting, the Board agreed to purchase for $556 an additional small lot at the corner of Ann and McQueen streets.

On September 11, 1953, the architectural firm of Sherlock Smith and Adams was selected to do the site work, and on January 8, 1954, a $36,300 contract was let for grading on Ann Street.

Montgomery Sertoma Club President H. S. Berman Jr. came to the March 12, 1954, meeting to present a letter to the Board asking that the new school be named Robert E. Lee High School. The Board postponed a vote "until the school is nearer completion."

On April 4, 1954, the Board voted to postpone the expected completion date of the school until July 30, 1954, "due to severe weather between June 29, 1953 and December 19, 1953." This delay was for only 15 days.

On July 14, 1954 Mr. Tim Carlton was named principal of the new school with an effective employment date of July 1, 1955. (The school had yet to be named)

On November 26, 1954, a second classroom unit was approved. Although not stated, this probably consisted of another 20 rooms with $505,850 approved for construction. Assistant Superintendent William Silas Garrett presented to the Board recommendations relative to establishing an attendance district for the new school. This was roughly to be north and east of Carter Hill Road and east of a line drawn northwardly to include the attendance districts of the following elementary schools: Forest Avenue, Highland Avenue, Capitol Heights Elementary, Morningview, Dalraida, Chisholm, and the new proposed school in Highland Gardens.

Also discussed at the November 26th meeting were several challenges

The Vision

The Robert E. Lee High School physical plant in 1955.

connected with the opening of the new school. The discussion resulted in a unanimous directive to the superintendent to write all then-enrolled 10th- and 11th-grade Lanier pupils residing in the new attendance area stating that they had the option of continuing at Lanier or attending the new school, which would be accredited as Lanier was. The students were required to make their choices, which, when approved by their parents or guardians, would be final.

The last item of business on November 26 concerned the school's name, and "on motion properly made and seconded, the Board named the new high school in memory of the distinguished southern leader and educator, Robert E. Lee."

On February 11, 1955, Lanier High School Principal Lee Douglas presented a $2,500 check to be used at Lee as start-up funds (new schools in this era received few funds from the Board to support administrative and instructional needs).

On March 19, the Board began employing and assigning teachers to Lee for the fall 1955 opening; a significant number were from Lanier.

On July 1, 1955, the Board approved the purchase and installation of basketball goals with an anticipated cost of $3,000 to $4,000. Another allocation was made for "grading and installation of grass" on the campus, apparently the last major Board action before Lee High School opened 66 days later. Interestingly, sixty years later, grass is still a sore point at Lee.

The stage was thus set for the opening of the school in September 1955.

DURING THE FIRST TWO decades of its existence, several additions were made to the school. The auditorium and band and choral rooms were completed by Bear Construction Company in 1964 at a cost of $500,000. The first play presented in the new auditorium was "Joey's Christmas" directed by drama teacher, Julia Crittenden. In this play, Joey was a young man who had experienced a loss of sight. In the opening scene, Joey was lying on a bed with a bandage over his eyes. As the new curtains opened, the on-stage microphone was knocked over and the noise caused Joey to rise up from

A 1,964-seat auditorium was added in 1964.

The patio area adjacent to the library, enjoyed by these early students, was removed when additions were made to the building.

his bed and pull away his bandage to see what had happened. It was an interesting beginning.

OTHER ADDITIONS TO THE campus over the years have included a mini-gym, a 16-classroom addition to the north of the rear wing, enclosure of the former patio area outside the cafeteria and extension of the east wall of the cafeteria to expand seating space, and a free-standing classroom unit to the north of the library. In the early 1970s, the sale of $1 raffle tickets raised $10,000 (the raffle prize was $1,000) to place window air-conditioning units in all classrooms.

By 1970, the enrollment had more than tripled to approximately 2,600 and Lee had become the largest three-grade high school in Alabama—larger than some of the state's colleges and universities. The faculty and staff had grown four times to 140 (and a student-faculty ratio of about 18:1).

Mr. Timothy C. Carlton, 1901–1975.

2

The First Principal

The Man and the Vision Meet in Timothy C. Carlton

By Clinton Carter

Robert E. Lee's first principal was Timothy Cox Carlton, who was approved by the Montgomery County Board of Education with an effective start date of July 1, 1955. His salary was set at $6,420 per year; however, prior to the beginning of the 1955–56 school year, all employees received a raise and Mr. Carlton's salary was increased to $7,640.

According to family tree information, Mr. Carlton was one of eight children of Goodson Cox Carlton and Emaline Miller Carlton of Jackson County, Alabama.

Mr. Carlton was born September 28, 1901, and died January 12, 1975. He is entombed beside his wife, Annie Earle Carlton (September 12, 1902–November 30, 1988), in the Mausoleum of Greenwood Cemetery at the corner of Lincoln Road and Highland Avenue in Montgomery. The Carltons had no children.

Mr. Carlton, as can be seen in photographs in the school's yearbook, was slightly less than six feet tall and somewhat portly. During school hours he wore a suit and tie and paid particular attention to keeping his shoes shined. In the summers he wore short-sleeved white dress shirts without a tie and exchanged his dress shoes for shoes with crepe soles to avoid foot pain from his constant walking around the campus.

Mrs. Carlton was a math teacher whose last assignment was at Goodwyn Junior High School. She depended on Mr. Carlton for almost everything in her life. He faithfully and without complaint shopped for their groceries and took all the washing and dry cleaning to Scott's Cleaners on Mt. Meigs Road every Friday, stopping along the way at the Union Bank branch to cash a check for $30 to $50 as his weekly spending money.

Mr. Carlton told me he had received less than twelve years of formal education, relying on his mother for extended schooling at home. He was a mathematics graduate of the University of Alabama and later received a master's in education from Peabody College at Vanderbilt University. He also attended seminars at Harvard University's School of Education.

Prior to moving to Montgomery, Mr. Carlton had taught in the rural schools of Jackson County and had served as principal of Vance High School. His began his career in Montgomery as a math teacher at Lanier. He then served first as principal of Catoma Elementary and later as principal of Capitol Heights Junior High before his promotion to the Lee position. He retired as principal of Lee at the end of June 1970.

I became Mr. Carlton's vice principal in July 1962, succeeding Mr. Lee Boone, who had been named principal of Capitol Heights Junior High after the promotion of Mr. T. A. Kirby to the position of assistant superintendent.

Lee High School's first vice principal, Lee Boone, left, was succeeded in 1962 by Clinton Carter, right (later Lee's second principal).

I can only surmise that my selection was based on the recommendation of Mr. Kirby and Mr. Jack Rutland, then principal of Goodwyn Junior High, both of whom I had served as "principal's helper."

Even before I officially assumed my duties at Lee, Mr. Carlton invited me to come to the campus for a grand tour and indoctrination into the Lee culture. I never saw anyone so proud of a position, and he instantly became a second father and a far-reaching influence on my life. Within a few months I had gained his trust and from that point forward was given complete authority to carry out my responsibilities and to be groomed as his replacement, whenever that time might come.

I am unable to put into words an explanation of his philosophy of life. I can only say that it was positive and included the cultivation of friendships with loyalty that could not be broken.

MR. CARLTON WAS OF the old school regarding discipline and manners. He could be ruthless when meting out punishment, but at the same time he took the repentant under his wing. Boys sent to the office for a paddling were greeted with the salutation, "Fresh Meat." Many Lee graduates can attest to these observations. The evidence of Mr. Carlton's caring spirit is typified by the special recognition given to Richard Jordan in this book.

Mr. Carlton was innovative when it came to solving many of the everyday problems that cropped up at the school, as evidenced by one example recalled by Nell Rushton McGilberry. She writes, "In 1957 or 1958 there was a third-floor window, overlooking the school entrance, that was constantly being broken. Mr. Carlton had it replaced numerous times, but it was always broken again soon after. Finally, he turned the responsibility for the window over to the Letter Club. If it were broken again, the Letter Club would have to replace it. I don't remember that the Letter Club had to replace it. When the word got around that the Letter Club was watching and responsible for the window, the window stayed intact!"

Nell's other memories of Mr. Carlton include his personal interest in thanking parents for some of the more mundane help they gave. She recalls that for many years when Mr. Carlton was principal of Capitol Heights her mother would bake cakes and take them to the school for teachers on the last teacher work day. When he was leaving Capitol Heights to become principal of Lee, he wrote Nell's mother a letter thanking her for all the "beautiful cakes you sent. They were even better than they looked. When Nell gets to senior high school, I am going to suggest to her teachers that they fail her every year so that we will [continue to] get cakes . . . Mrs. Carlton and I enjoyed, as usual, the one that I took home."

Continuing her recollection, Nell recalled that before she was old enough to attend Capitol Heights her brothers would talk about Mr. Carlton's "electric paddle" and she always tried to imagine what an "electric paddle" looked like.

She stated that "Mr. Carlton had the best interests of all students uppermost in his mind. He expected students to toe the line, but he understood that students faltered at times. One of his sayings was, 'They all have to go over fool's hill at some time.' His main concern was that the students would learn from their mistakes and become better. There were many times that a student did something 'stupid' and would find himself facing police and court problems. It was not at all uncommon for Mr. Carlton to intervene with the authorities and ask to have the student turned over to him for discipline and guidance. Usually, his request was granted."

Dr. Haywood Bartlett, a close friend of Mr. Carlton's, endowed a scholarship fund in honor of his aunt Bessie and he, along with Mr. Carlton and the Rev. Louis Armstrong, were the first trustees. To my knowledge, all recipients of loans from this fund were Lee graduates.

Mr. Carlton was a devoted member of the Montgomery Lions Club and served as its president in 1950. Mr. Carlton never missed his Lions Club meeting on Fridays. He made it clear to me that since both of us could not be gone from the school at the same time, he would not sponsor me as a Lion until he retired. Meanwhile, he "invited" me to assist him with manning the gates for the annual Blue-Gray game at Cramton Bowl on Christmas Day and I did so. After his retirement, he sponsored me as a Lion. He was also an active member of First Baptist Church, Shriners, Toastmasters, and the Blue-Gray Football Association.

Everyone has idiosyncrasies and Tim Carlton was no exception. He never passed a door frame without backing up to it and using it as a scratching post. He was known for smoking Tampa Nugget cigars, sometimes at his desk and in the building during the summer lull. It was not unusual to find a soggy cigar left on the check-in counter in the school office. I recall his having smoked nine cigars during one football game. Empty cigar boxes were saved and used by the cashiers at athletic events. He constantly flicked tobacco bits onto the dash of his car when smoking and the mess it made never seemed to bother him.

He had a bit of disdain for most military personnel. Perhaps it was because of the heavy enrollment of students whose fathers were stationed at Gunter who had problems understanding the culture of a Southern school and the absolute authority with which principals oversaw their schools. I was usually invited to sit in with Mr. Carlton when he dealt with parents and others who had come to complain. The most memorable of these was a visit by the Commander of Air University and his aide. The commander wanted Mr. Carlton to allow a survey of boys to determine interest in Scouting. He was refused because Mr. Carlton allowed no interference with instructional time. When the general protested, Mr. Carlton cupped his hand, slapped it on the desk and said, "You listen to me, *Lieutenant.* You are not going to do a survey in this school." The aide and I slid down in our chairs and the meeting ended.

Mr. Carlton had small hands and I can still visualize his cupped right hand slapping that desk.

On another occasion, the son of a high-ranking State Trooper caused a problem. Mr. Carlton picked up the phone and told the Trooper to come to the school. He showed up a few minutes later. I don't recall the problem the son was causing, but I do remember Mr. Carlton telling the Trooper Dad that his son "had a sorry streak down his back."

THE CARLTONS LIVED IN a modest house on Wildwood Drive. The house was furnished with Victorian-era furniture and the windows were treated with drapes and sheers. The only air conditioning was one small window unit in the bedroom. The yard was well-kept and mowed by Mr. John Pickett, head custodian at Lee. Mr. Carlton would pick him up at his home in north Montgomery on Saturday mornings to do the yard chores. Numerous plants and shrubs added to the attractiveness of the yard, attesting to Mr. Carlton's appreciation for horticulture.

Mr. Carlton was sensitive to pain suffered by those whom he knew. He was constantly attending funerals and visiting the homes of relatives of the deceased. When a person close to the Lee family passed away, he ordered flowers and in almost every instance sent a telegram that he dictated to Mrs. Louise Smyth. Although brief, the telegram always ended with "Your loss is our loss."

Mrs. Louise Smyth was his personal bookkeeper in addition to serving as the registrar at Lee. She maintained his checkbook and wrote checks for all his bills in preparation for his signature, all on school time.

Mrs. Smyth was recognized in the May 20, 1964, *Stars and Bars*:

> Mrs. Louise Smyth is the school secretary and practically the hub of all office activity. She was a member of the first office staff that came

Mrs. Louise Smyth, secretary and bookkeeper, followed Principal Carlton from Capitol Heights Junior High School when Lee opened in 1955.

to Lee when it opened nine years ago. Before coming to Lee, she served as secretary at Capitol Heights Junior High School for eight years. Mrs. Smyth is loved by all the students. Her only comment about the students is "I love them all, both bad and good."

Following home football games, Mr. Carlton went by the school and visited briefly with the coaches. His social engagements included attending events of Toastmasters and the Lions Club. He also could be found at Sadie's Deli on Coliseum Boulevard on most Saturday mornings where he would have breakfast with a few of the Lee supporters. His favorite pub was located on Fairview Avenue across from the Clover Theatre (now the Capri), where on some evenings he would meet friends and have a couple of vodkas with water on the side. His close friends addressed him as "Timmy."

The local Coca-Cola Bottling Company had a fishing boat in Panama City. During the summer Mr. Carlton and several others, including his good friend and Coca-Cola employee Foster Goodwin, would go down for a couple of days of deep-sea fishing with a good deal of partying included.

Mayor Earl James was a good friend of Mr. Carlton. They had worked together at Capitol Heights Junior High and the mayor frequently came by the school to visit. I was once invited to join them for a ride out the Atlanta Highway. It was terribly hot, but the mayor turned off the air conditioning in his car and had us roll the windows down. He observed that he could not be seen in an air-conditioned environment by his supporters and the open windows allowed him to wave at his constituents.

Students are inclined to give nicknames to administrators and teachers. During the 1960s, Mr. Carlton was known as "Top Cat" and I was known as "Deputy Dog," names taken from TV cartoon characters.

Nothing interfered with his lunch time at Lee. The lunchroom manager put a table in the pantry and it became the site of lunches for him, the assistant principal, and occasionally community leaders who had received a special invitation. The Herff-Jones representative who sold class rings and invitations to Lee students presented a plaque reading "Mr. Tim's Pantry" and it was attached to the wall. The decision to eat away from the student body could have been a simple case of privacy or it could have been driven by the fact that Mr. Carlton's hands shook from some malady that never received a diagnosis. Whatever the cause, most Lee students were aware of it.

Mr. Carlton began experiencing health problems in the mid-1960s, including issues related to the heart and kidneys. Several surgeries took their toll and diminished his stamina toward the end of his tenure.

The community gave him a new Ford sedan (his first vehicle with air conditioning) at his retirement in May 1970. The Montgomery County Board of Education subsequently named the Lee auditorium in his honor.

Perhaps his spirit and his sense of loyalty to the school and appreciation for parent and community support are best summed up in the article he wrote in the May 20, 1956, *Montgomery Advertiser*.

> It is natural and fitting at this time of year to take a backward glance and check up on our mileage, for we have really come a long way since September 6. To open a new school is no chore, but a gigantic and challenging job accomplished at Robert E. Lee by the united and untiring effort of the administrative staff, the faculty, the students, the patrons, and hundreds of other friends of education in Montgomery.
>
> We are humbly grateful to all who had any part, however large or small in the founding and the nourishing of the institution that is to be a stepping stone to higher learning for the youth of this community for years to come.
>
> We are mindful of and appreciative of the elementary schools and their faculties who make the first imprint of formal education upon our prospective students, and of the junior high school teachers who, with patience and skill, strive to gear these pupils to good study habits and scholastic zeal that will adjust them to senior high routines.
>
> Many of our students came to us this year from Sidney Lanier. It was not easy to break away from a school, which they all loved, to enroll in a brand new school with no traditions behind it. They made the break, and they are happy here although they are still bound to Lanier with many ties of friendship and many happy memories. To all who helped them arrive at their present milestone, we are indebted. It remains for Robert

The First Principal

Fred Guy, left, and James Bozeman began their careers at Lee High School as teachers and assistant principals in the Carlton era. Both would later serve as principals of the school.

E. Lee High to take up the task so nobly begun by other schools and project these fine boys and girls further on their way to successful living.

In 1964, Mr. Carlton received the Medal of Honor from the Montgomery Chamber of Commerce in recognition of his meritorious years of service in the field of education. The school newspaper, reporting on this event, stated, "All Lee High School is surely proud of our principal's outstanding work and is appreciative of the rich experience he has gained which enable him to serve so understandingly and efficiently as an administrator."

From Tim Carlton I gained the foundation that enabled me to carry forward his vision for a great school. Succeeding principals for the next generation carried on this torch, including particularly Fred Guy and James Bozeman, who began their careers as teachers and assistant principals during Mr. Carlton's decade and a half as Lee principal.

3

'Red & White' or 'Blue & Gray'

A New Beginning and New Traditions

EDITOR'S NOTE: Few are granted the privilege of knowingly establishing a tradition or creating a custom. Thus, when Lee High School was founded in 1955, its first faculty, staff, and students had a rare opportunity of establishing a number of traditions which were expected to be associated with such an educational institution—and a few others which just happened to spring up. Even as these and other practices evolved, Lee High partisans knew that "[t]radition is a guide and is not a jailer," as American novelist W. Somerset Maugham once put it.

BY CLINTON CARTER

Coach Jim Chafin, a member of the Lee staff from its opening, recalled in a 2014 interview that the first meeting with students who were zoned to attend Lee was held in the spring of 1955 in the auditorium of Capitol Heights Junior High School.

THE NICKNAME AND COLORS

According to Coach Chafin, two things most needed to be decided—the school colors and the nickname. The nickname was first with "Generals" receiving the most votes. The decision on color was not without debate. Some wanted blue and gray, but many resisted on the basis that these colors were not colorful enough. After much discussion a majority voted for red and white. We learned later that these were the colors head football coach Tom Jones wanted because he thought they would make it easier for his players to "hide the ball," when that was desirable! Some objected because red and white were Cloverdale's colors, but Cloverdale was a junior high and it was concluded that there was thus no conflict.

Lee students Marie (Little) Parma, Alice (Bach) Robinson, and Rod Lide were present at the Capitol Heights meeting and share their memories:

> MARIE PARMA: "Excitement was in the air at the meeting of students who would attend the new Lee High School opening in the fall of 1955. The auditorium of Capitol Heights Junior High School was crowded and the noise level lively as topics such as school colors, nickname, and school mascot were being decided. Several colors were mentioned: blue and gray, red and gray, gold and gray, and red and white. When the vote was taken, red and white was chosen. Three names emerged for the 'nickname': Rebels, Confederates, and Generals. The popular choice was Generals. We had the opportunity to hear from the new coaches. There was a feeling of unity to be in the first student body of the new 'eastside' school. . .a feeling of excitement to make decisions that would be long-lasting. This

Future Lee students voting for "Generals" as the new school's nickname, at a meeting at Capitol Heights Junior High in the spring of 1955.

gathering of students allowed us in a small way to take ownership of the school that would become our alma mater. We took that responsibility seriously and with great pride, honor, and respect."

ROD LIDE: "I recall a number of us wanted gold and Confederate gray as the school colors. Gold and gray, very Southern, very Robert E. Lee. I also remember Coach Chafin suggesting before the vote that we needed to pick a color scheme that would 'last' and he suggested red and white."

ALICE (BACH) ROBINSON: "My first recollection is the feeling of excitement that was in the auditorium. To think these new students who were to be the first graduating class of Lee High School would have any say about anything was somewhat overwhelming! We were very excited to know we would be attending classes in a new modern building. We were 'coached' somewhat on the colors to select because of the ease of buying football uniforms in those particular colors. We wrote our color choices on a piece of paper and passed it to the end of the row. To be able to attend school in the part of Montgomery where I lived was a thrill. Also it was nice to be a part of a smaller student body. There was a friendlier atmosphere among the students than I had experienced at Lanier because it was so huge. My senior year at Lee was a very happy time and I am so thankful I was able to be a part of the first graduating class."

The Scabbard

Once the school opened, the yearbook became known as *The Scabbard*. This may have been the result of the poem by Abram Joseph Ryan that appears inside the 1956 debut yearbook. An excerpt reads:

> THE SWORD OF ROBERT E. LEE
> Forth, from its scabbard, pure and bright,
> Flashed the sword of Lee
> Far in the front of the deadly fight,
> High oe'r the brave in the cause of Right,
> Its stainless sheen, like a beacon light, . . .

The award-winning debut edition of the Lee High School yearbook.

> . . . Nor purer sword led braver band,
> Nor braver bled for a brighter land,
> Nor brighter land had a cause so grand,
>   Nor a cause a chief like Lee!

The Scabbard won the 1956 Alabama Sweepstakes Award for best annual—a remarkable accomplishment for a high school in its inaugural year.

THE *Stars and Bars*

In the early years and continuing until around 1970 the school newspaper carried the masthead "Stars and Bars." With an increasing number of African American students the masthead was gradually redesigned until the cannons and the Confederate flag no longer appeared.

The following article appeared in the November 20, 1964, *Stars and Bars*:

> On the first page of every Lee student newspaper appears the masthead *Stars and Bars*. This banner, drawn by Alice Bach in 1955, has become symbolic of everything for which this school stands. Some would say we have hung our banner on a lost cause for which a war was fought. It is more than that. It is a heritage of the land in which we live. It stands for the great men this land has produced, men like Robert E. Lee or Jefferson Davis.

There is nothing to identify the author of the above article. One would assume it was one of the staff of the paper. It was written three months after the first African American students were enrolled.

The "Alma Mater"

The "Alma Mater" was written by Mrs. Annie Laurie Lindsey, Lee's first Dean of Girls and Director of Activities. Mrs. Lindsey had been an English teacher at Capitol Heights Junior High. Although she composed two verses, the second verse became the one students most often sang:

> 1. Lee High to thee in joyous lay we pledge our steadfast will to bear thy ensign always high, thy lofty hopes fulfill. The years will pass, as years will do, and class by class depart. Alma Mater, as they leave thee, hold thy love in every heart.
> 2. Lee High, we honor thee today as always we shall do; when e'er our thoughts on thee are turned, our hearts imbibe anew. The sweetest draft from purest springs of knowledge, deep and clear, Alma Mater, nearer, dearer, by thy spirit year by year.

During the first few decades of the school's existence, those words became familiar to all Lee High students; and they sang them accurately on a number of occasions throughout each academic year—most often at football game halftimes but also at certain assemblies and on special occasions. Such practice is not so common in public high schools in this century.

The Flag

In Lee High's earliest years, the Confederate battle flag—often misunderstood as the flag of the Confederate States of America—played a prominent role on campus and off. A battle flag dominated the east wall of the gymnasium until 1970, by which time change in the racial makeup of the school had made it a point of confusion and contention. Photographs of the band in 1955–56 show this flag on the bass drum and it was carried as a part of the color guard. The flag was proudly displayed by students at athletic events, appeared in various publications of the school, and could be found attached to the walls in various classrooms, not to mention on student artifacts and in and on the automobiles of the few who had them.

"Dixie"

As could be expected, the rousing song "Dixie" became the fight song of Robert E. Lee High School. It was played at every pep rally and at all public appearances of the band, even when they were in competition in northern states. Along with the Confederate flag, "Dixie" faded away with the increasing enrollment of African Americans and the band substituted "Waiting for the Robert E. Lee."

The Lee High School Ring

According to an article in an early issue of the *Stars and Bars*, the ring was selected by a committee of 20 students. Their engraved-gold design featured on one side a rendering of the school building above two apparently Confederate flags and the first two digits of the year of graduation, as well as rampant stars—all above "EST. 1955" in block letters on a scroll, and on the other side, the second two digits of the graduating year above the Lee statue, which is surrounded by laurel and other celebratory greenery, its base hovering above the word "GENERALS." The centerpiece of the ring was a red stone, surrounded by "ROBERT E. LEE HIGH SCHOOL *MONTGOMERY*." The student's initials were engraved in script on the inside of the ring. The *Stars and Bars* reported that some 48 seniors (about a third of the class) bought the rings that year.

The Coat of Arms

The Lee High School Coat of Arms, based on that of the Robert E.

Lee Family, was carved by Major Walter Clifton Cummins and carries the Latin inscription, *"ne incautus futuri"*—"let us not be unconcerned about the future." Major Cummins [1907–77], is buried in Greenwood Cemetery. He served in the U.S. Army Air Corps, retiring at Maxwell AFB in 1946. He was a skilled woodcarver and crafted the Altar Rail for St. James Methodist Church on South Court Street, together with figures of the twelve disciples. He also carved the coat of arms for the Museum of Fine Arts. Apparently, he crafted and donated the Lee coat of arms merely as an act of charity, for he had no known connections with the school. The coat of arms originally hung on the south wall of the lobby at the Ann Street entrance to the school, but was moved when that wall was demolished to make way for the entrance to the auditorium that came on line in 1964. Its location as of 2015 was unknown.

ROBERT E. LEE LIKENESSES

In addition to the Lee statue (see Chapter 5), a portrait of Lee was presented to the school in 1955 by Mr. Robert E. Steiner Jr. of Montgomery. The photograph in a gold frame revealed a full-length view of its subject and was hung in the principal's office after its presentation. And a bust of Lee was given by Mr. William P. Arrington of Montgomery, an ardent admirer of Lee and a friend of Robert E. Lee High School.

The May 20, 1964, *Stars and Bars* reported that a second portrait of Lee had been donated to the school. "Warm appreciation goes to Mr. Fred Bear from the students of Lee High School for his help in acquiring a lovely 24x32 inch portrait of Robert E. Lee that hangs in the lobby of the new auditorium," it was reported. "The picture, beautifully tinted and exquisitely framed, shows General Lee as an educator. The original portrait, painted by Miss Hattie Burdette, hangs in the chapel of Washington and Lee University, the Alma Mater of the builders of Robert E. Lee High School. To enhance the charm of the portrait of Lee, the student council recently placed beneath it a stately shrub in a gleaming brass urn."

That portrait has been restored and hangs in the school lobby.

4

Life at Lee in the Early Years

By Clinton Carter

How the School Was Organized and Run

Given current technology and the many innovations that have become commonplace in the operation of modern schools, it is amazing how little of either was available to the first students and faculty at Robert E. Lee High School in the fall of 1955. Amazing also are the changes that have evolved regarding conduct, dress, and other rules that governed the lives of students as they attended classes and engaged in activities both at school and at school-sponsored events off-campus.

The Faculty and Staff

The total administrative/supervisory staff when the school opened in 1955 consisted of the principal, one vice principal, one counselor, a director for activities, and two secretaries. The 35-member faculty (giving the new school a student-faculty ratio of about 23:1) consisted of mostly highly qualified and effective individuals who will be listed and described in Chapter 6.

The State of Technology

All student records were recorded manually, entries being made in pen or pencil. This included permanent record cards and attendance and grade reports. Student class schedules were handled entirely by head secretary Louise Smyth. A matrix containing each teacher's name and daily schedule was written on a poster board. Space was left for Mrs. Smyth to tally the number of students assigned to each class as a control mechanism. She entered a class schedule for each student on a printed 3 x 5 card, making a duplicate for office use. So personal was this process that she and the administrators could consider a student's individual strengths and weaknesses in assigning them to various teachers.

As previously noted, schools in the 1950s were on their own in securing equipment and supplies. The $2,500 donated to Lee by the Lanier principal, along with community support and modest student fees for certain courses, provided the only revenue to maintain the athletics and instructional programs. Once the football program gained success, some of its gate receipts were utilized to buy basic materials such as copier paper. The newspaper staff raised funds by selling ads and operating a supply store.

There was one spirit duplicator, or mimeograph, to serve the entire school. It was kept in a closet in the main office and closely monitored by the administrators. Teachers wrote or typed their own exams and other handouts on a master which was then attached to the drum of the machine and hand-cranked to produce copies. Some students say they can still recall the intoxicating smell produced by "the ink" used in the transfer process.

The school secretaries used manual typewriters, and all typewriters in the business education classes were manuals.

There were only six telephones in the building. All were rotary dial. Both secretaries had a phone. The principal, vice principal, and lunchroom manager each had a phone, and there was a phone in the coaches' office. Calls could not be transferred from one phone to another. For example, calls to the principal were answered by one of the secretaries who then went to his office to tell him he had a call. When the principal needed a secretary, he pushed a button under his desk and a buzzer sounded at the secretary's desk. Pay phones were available for students in the front and gym lobbies.

Food Preparation: One Meal a Day

Mrs. Mattie Bell Cook, the lunchroom manager, was an excellent chef, but hell on wheels with most students, teachers, and her workers. At the end of a school term, it was customary for the lunchroom manager to give

Lunch in the early days, always accompanied by a student-led prayer.

remaining perishable food items to her workers. Mrs. Cook once divided up these items and then discovered a worker had taken a pork chop without permission. She gathered all workers around a large trash container and required them to dump in the flour and meal she had distributed, after which she doused them with water to render them useless.

All Mrs. Cook's produce was delivered fresh each morning. There was no walk-in refrigerator or freezer, nor were there any deep-fat fryers. All meats were baked or broiled. Lunches consisted of one standard meal, usually a meat, two vegetables, a homemade yeast roll, a dessert, and a carton of milk. No variations were allowed. Neither students nor faculty were allowed to take any food item from the cafeteria. Teachers were required to sit with their students at assigned tables. Neither students nor faculty were allowed to bring outside drinks or food into the cafeteria; students were not allowed to bring food or drinks into the building at all. There were no vending machines for students. One drink machine was located in the teachers' lounge, dispensing only Coca-Colas in six-ounce bottles. No one was allowed to take a bottle from this room.

Other Creature Comforts

By 1962, the principal's office was still the only air-conditioned spot in the school, and it was thanks to a used window unit salvaged from the razed courthouse and donated by the Montgomery County Commission. Over the next few years several more window units were added to office areas. The coaches procured a unit for their office, but when Mr. Carlton discovered they had done this, he chewed them out and threatened to have the unit removed.

All classroom floors were genuine oak, kept clean by the use of large dust mops impregnated with an oily substance. There were no carpets or rugs in the building.

Students had little privacy. Each had an assigned locker in the hallways and always subject to unannounced search by school officials. Student lockers were not rented, but students were required to use combination locks sold by the school at $2 each. A book with all the combinations was kept in the school vault. We bought locks from willing sellers at the end of the school year for $1 and recycled them for the next term.

The secretaries in the front office dispensed aspirin to students upon their request, no questions asked.

Personnel, Clothing, and Pregnancy

The African American custodial personnel were wonderful, caring persons who were treated with respect, but, as was the custom of the day, they did not drink from the water fountains in the hallways, nor did they use any toilets, except for the one assigned to them near the boiler room. They were provided lunches, but did not eat in the cafeteria.

Until after the mid-1960s, African Americans did not attend football games at Cramton Bowl. An exception was made for one of our custodians, Mr. John Pickett, who came on occasion and sat in the north end zone area. There was no rule barring African Americans. It was just one of those things during this time period.

Female teachers wore dresses and male teachers and administrators wore ties, usually with coats. One teacher came to school wearing slacks and Secretary Louise Smyth sent her directly home to change. Female students usually wore dresses or skirts with blouses. Dressy slacks were permitted, but females could not wear jeans, shorts, or culottes. The hair of male students could not cover the back of the shirt collar. The yearbook for the school year 1962–63 does not show a single male student whose ears could not be seen.

Girls who became pregnant were required to drop out of school, although I don't recall one who had to be told to do so. It was just understood. Teachers who became pregnant, all married of course, left their jobs in the very early stages of their pregnancy. There was no maternity leave with pay.

Married students were required to "register" with the office, and I only recall one student (a girl) who was allowed to remain on the roll after marriage. Married students could not be cheerleaders, nor hold elected positions, nor be "featured" in the yearbook.

Books, Cheap Technology, and Chalk Dust

Students purchased all their own books. The Anders bookstore in downtown Montgomery was a source for used textbooks and others were passed from person to person.

With the exception of chalkboards, there were no teaching aids such as overhead projectors or screens in the classrooms. The school had a few record players, 16-mm film projectors, and tape recorders that teachers could check out of the library.

Teachers were constantly reminded not to allow students to beat the dust out of chalkboard erasers on the walls outside exit doors!

The Role and Rule of Discipline

Boys who wanted to settle a dispute by fighting were sometimes given boxing gloves and allowed to square off in the gym and pummel each other. Physical punishment was the order of the day for minor infractions. Every male administrator and teacher had a paddle and they used these paddles totally at their discretion, deciding when and where to administer the punishment.

Students who were suspended or expelled were told by the principal or vice principal to clean out his or her locker and hit the road. No letters or phone calls to parents were required and therefore were rarely used. No "due process" was involved.

Students who were significantly behind academically, coupled with a history of disciplinary problems, could expect a letter in the summer informing them not to return the next school year.

Students new to Montgomery and who had not come to register during the summer months were isolated on the first day of school. After a severe scolding, each was interviewed and his or her records reviewed before clearance to enroll was granted. Potential troublemakers were sent away pending further investigation into their pasts; some were not allowed to enroll.

Smoking was allowed, but only in the restrooms. I don't recall much evidence that many girls were smoking. On the other hand, the boys' restrooms were constantly filled with smoke and littered with cigarette butts. Most coaches either smoked or used chewing tobacco. They chewed at practices, at games, and in the coaches' office, where they used paper cups as spittoons. As previously mentioned, Mr. Carlton smoked cigars in his office, in the hallways during the summer months, and at football games.

Football Games

At that time, there were no classes or programs to serve special needs students and there were no recognized competitive high school sports or coaches for female students. But boys' sports—especially football—were hugely significant, both within the schools and in the community.

Today we are concerned about violence at high school sporting events. So were we then. It was fairly common in the early '60s for fistfights to break out at football games in Cramton Bowl, usually under the east stands. Other problems included firecrackers and thrown bottles. At an out-of-town football game some of the home team fans threw bottles at the band bus and broke several windows.

Fights between Lee students and opposing fans at places between Montgomery and the game site were not uncommon. On one occasion, several Lee students became involved in a brawl at a bus terminal in Sylacauga on the way back from a game. Two were identified and as precondition to their attendance at future games were required to hire an off-duty police officer to sit with them at Cramton Bowl, even accompanying them to the restroom.

A typical football crowd at Cramton Bowl. You had to be there to understand it.

Every faculty member was required to work at football games and other athletic events. Female teachers sold tickets and male teachers took them up at the gates. At halftime, the principal or his assistant would go from gate to gate and give each faculty member a dime as payment; this bonus was increased to a quarter beginning in 1962.

The week prior to the annual Lee-Lanier football game was a total academic waste. Students held impromptu pep rallies in the halls and in the cafeteria. Pep rallies on the Atlanta Highway on the night before the game stopped all traffic, with students spilling across traffic lanes. One pep rally near the Dairy Queen on Mt. Meigs Road attracted so many unruly fans that the police department used its K-9 unit for control, causing some students to climb on top of a canopy.

Pranks by both Lee and Lanier students were common. School employees and the police department stayed on-site at both schools until well after midnight on the night before the game. It was common for Lanier fans to paint the statue of General Lee, once thwarted because we had covered it with petroleum jelly. Plastic sheeting was also used from time to time. Lanier students once came into the auditorium during a school day and spraypainted "LANIER" on the wall. Lee students once sneaked into the Lanier building on a school day and made their way to the top front floor where they unfurled a banner reading "LEE" out of a window. On another occasion, Lee students planted winter grass seed on Lanier's front lawn spelling out "LEE" in large letters. The seeds sprouted with the first rain, making it impossible to conceal the letters. A "LANIER" metal sign was once chained to the fence along Ann Street.

Lee and Lanier supporters tried to out-do each other at the big game. The half-time show was spectacular each year. Lee once had a float in the shape of the State Capitol building (previously used in a gubernatorial campaign).

Tickets to the Lee-Lanier game were sold at ticket booths at Paterson Field in August with a 10-ticket limit. Some fans spent the night in the parking lot to be guaranteed their tickets. All 24,000 tickets were sold within hours, and I believe we could have doubled this number if the bowl could have accommodated the crowd. Pep rallies in the gym could only be described in today's terms as awesome. There is no way to describe the atmosphere unless you were there.

Graduation

All graduates wore the same white gowns and the same color tassels and collars. The rationale was that all students having met graduation requirements should be treated equally on graduation night. Few schools today present the actual diplomas during the ceremony, but in those days Lee did, and they were rolled into scrolls and tied with a red ribbon. The manual arts shop made special wooden containers with numbered holes to keep the diplomas in the correct order for handing out.

On-time attendance at graduation rehearsal was required. Violators sat in the audience on graduation night and picked up their diplomas at the school the following day.

A formal, dignified ceremony was expected and the audience cooperated. Individual applause, celebrations, hoots and hollers, or other raucous behavior as individuals were presented their diplomas might well have caused school officials to stop the ceremony and demand silence. That despite the fact that Lee commencement ceremonies during the first decade were held in the same arena—Garrett Coliseum—which hosted rodeos, pop concerts, demolition derbies, athletic events, and the annual Central Alabama Fair.

A Fast First Year

Lee High's first school year opened on September 6, 1955, with some 35 faculty members, a principal, vice principal, secretary, lunchroom manager, and four custodians.

Of the almost 800 students, 345 were sophomores who had transferred in from junior high schools in Lee's new attendance zone. Most of the 232 juniors and 173 seniors had transferred in from Lanier High School.

THE SCHOOL BOARD VISITS

On September 20, members of the Montgomery County school board toured the school for the first time, at the invitation of the Parent-Teacher Association.

W.O.W. FLAG PRESENTATION

On September 23—at the first-ever school assembly, the Woodmen of the World presented an American flag. According to the October 14 *Stars and Bars*, "An assembly was held outside in front of the school where newly elected Student Council officers were presented: Johnny Andrews, president; Sarah Burson, vice-president; Charles Jones, secretary; and Jan Gregory, treasurer. Immediately after the introduction, the band played 'America' and Dalton Guthrie gave the Bible reading. A prayer was given by Mr. H. L. Heaton, who was also the guest speaker. At the raising of the flag, the band played the 'Star Spangled Banner,' after which the students and guests recited the Pledge of Allegiance. The ceremony was brought to a close by the playing of 'America the Beautiful.'"

LEE'S FIRST PARADE

The first-ever Lee High School parade down Dexter Avenue occurred in October, as the October 14 *Stars and Bars* duly noted:

> The parade was an answer to everyone's questions. Montgomery was looking for something new, . . . different, bold, and colorful [and they got it, cheering] when "General Robert E. Lee," in his grey uniform trimmed

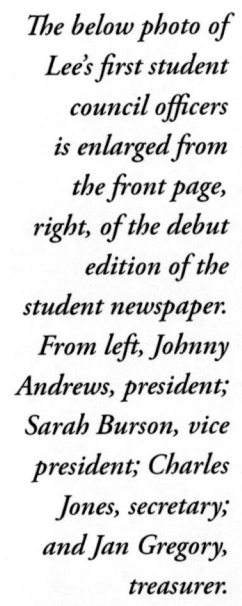

The below photo of Lee's first student council officers is enlarged from the front page, right, of the debut edition of the student newspaper. From left, Johnny Andrews, president; Sarah Burson, vice president; Charles Jones, secretary; and Jan Gregory, treasurer.

in red, led the parade . . . and he rode his horse well. The band followed . . . The drilling and summer practice really paid off. People were saying, "You know, Lee has some band!" The red and white uniforms with "Robert E. Lee" on the sleeves really were colorful and smart looking. The cheerleaders followed [the band], dressed in white sweaters which were trimmed in red and while L's. Their white skirts were lined with red. The cheerleaders looked pretty and were full of school spirit as they rode along in red and white convertibles. The student body backed the parade whole-heartedly. Many students decorated cars and rode in the parade, and many others were onlookers as they mingled with the crowd."

STUDENT NEWSPAPER FIRST ISSUE

The front page of the inaugural issue of the *Stars and Bars*, dated October 14, 1955, featured the student election, the W.O.W flag presentation, two references to Lee band activities on- and off-campus, the parade referenced above, and General Lee astride Traveller.

The editorial page included a commendation on recent displays of school spirit by Lee students; a message of appreciation from the Student Council President Johnny Andrews; an essay on a "Typical Lee Student," written by Melvin Urk; a flag-raising "MOMENT, occasioned by WOW's gift; and a short article headlined: "Students Extend Cordial Welcome to All Teachers at Lee . . ." The "Features" section on page 3 focused on the first school party of the year, the cheerleaders, and Tri-Hi-Y News. The remaining pages of the eight-page issue reported on "salutes" to two students; a "Report from Washington" by Lee student John Holleman, who had served as a page at the U.S. Capitol; the Latin Club's holding its first meeting of the year; and football coverage—easily the dominant focus of news in the paper with three pages devoted to it, a harbinger of coverage to come.

OFFICIAL DEDICATION OF THE SCHOOL

On December 11, Mr. Carlton presided as Robert E. Lee High School was finally and formally dedicated, 96 days after its Ann Street doors were opened to students. After several musical selections by the Lee Marching Band and an invocation by Dr. Henry A. Parker, pastor of the First Baptist

U.S. Senator Lister Hill speaking at the official dedication of the school in December 1955.

Church, the Glee Club sang and the Superintendent of Education Dr. C. M. Dannelly introduced the speaker for the occasion, U.S. Senator Lister Hill, one of the most respected men in Washington, well known for his knowledge of health and educational matters. To conclude the occasion, the glee club sang "America, Our Heritage," followed by a vocal benediction. Mary Louise Mills was the accompanist for the group.

THE FIRST GRADUATES

That first winter and spring of 1955–56, were perceived as a blur no doubt by many Lee students, especially the seniors awaiting graduation (144 of the 173 seniors who started the year did graduate). In a May 20, 1956, special "Cap and Gown" edition of the *Montgomery Advertiser*, captioned photos of graduates of Montgomery area high schools were included along with various articles related to local schools. It was noted that some 38 percent of Lee's graduating class would be entering college, with Auburn and Huntingdon attracting the largest numbers. Several others had chosen business colleges and schools of nursing. Some planned to end their formal education to become (or remain) married, while others announced engagement and wedding plans for the coming summer. Several of the young men reported that they were planning to enter military service and others simply planned to seek openings in the world of business.

The newspaper insert further reported that scholarships had been awarded to Lee students Johnny Andrews, Sue Waters, Donna Wyatt, Kathy Panhorst, and JoAnn Lewis. It was noted that music scholarships had been awarded to five members of the marching band and athletic awards to four football players and several baseball stars; other scholarships were pending.

At the May 18 assembly, trophies had been presented to cheerleaders by the athletic department for their outstanding service to the school. Recipients of sterling silver megaphones were: Ida Grimes, Alice Bach, Jerry Drinkard, Frances Goode, Dane Thompson, Patsy Flournoy, Mary Ann Pugh, Kitty Salter, Virginia Brophy, and Janice Canterbury.

The first baccalaureate exercises were held on Sunday, May 27. However, the students handed diplomas later that day at commencement were not the first graduates of Robert E. Lee High School; that distinction went to a group of four students who received their diplomas at the end of the first semester of the 1955–56 school year. Thereby Charles A. Kamburis became the very first Lee graduate, because his name came first on the alphabetical list used for the purpose. He still resides in Montgomery and is well known for his affiliation with Charles Anthony's "The Pub" Restaurant on Chantilly Parkway. The other three students graduated at that first mid-term were Paul Reeder, Robert Sims, and Bobby Wyatt.

5

Flashing Forward in Five-Year Increments

EDITOR'S NOTE: Among the many noteworthy events of the first decade of Robert E. Lee High School's history, two stand out because of their historic significance, their apparent connection, and their uniqueness as once-in-a-lifetime occurrences. The first was the relocation in 1960 of the statue of General Robert E. Lee from the intersection of Madison Avenue, Mt. Meigs Road, and Ann Street to in front of the school. The second, five years later, during the 1964–65 school year, was the arrival of the first African American students, both sides in the integration debate remaining silent, eventually acquiescing quietly in the desegregation of Lee High School.

Dedication of the Lee Statue, 1960

BY CLINTON CARTER

The statue of Robert E. Lee now standing in front of the school has an interesting history. It was constructed by the W. H. Mullins Company of Salem, Ohio, for erection in 1908 at Lee Place off Madison Avenue, in the new Capitol Heights residential area. Catalog material reveals that the statue was constructed of sheet copper with antique bronze finish. A photograph from the company's catalog shows the seven-foot statue mounted on a much taller pedestal than that of today. Records have not been located to indicate whether the taller pedestal was used or whether it was only a part of the sales catalog, since statues of Lee may also

Inset: The Lee statue was first erected at Lee Place off Madison Avenue in 1908. Below: By 1950, it had been moved to near the intersection of Madison and Ann Street, on a shorter pedestal.

have been made for other locations.

The statue was unveiled on June 12, 1908, in a ceremony conducted by the Joint Committee of Confederate Organizations of Montgomery. A parade preceded the ceremony, consisting of a detail of mounted police, the Grand Marshal and aides, a band, carriages containing committees, speakers, and ladies, Camp Lomax U.C.V., Camp Falkner U.C.V., and Camp Holtzclaw U.S.C.V., state, county, and city officials, military, and other carriages.

The parade route was highly organized, and according to the program, moved west along Madison Avenue to Vickers Street, thence along Vickers Street to Lee Circle for the ceremony.

State Archivist Dr. Thomas M. Owen chaired the event. The program included Confederate selections by a band, invocation, the formal presentation of the statue to the City of Montgomery with Mayor William M. Teague accepting, an address by Judge Thomas Goode Jones, and a salute by the Montgomery Field Artillery.

The program included two tributes to Lee: a poem by an unnamed writer praising "the tall exemplar / Of a grand, historic race" whom "Honor followed as his shadow," and another by Benjamin Harvey Hill identifying him as "a foe without hate; a friend without treachery; a soldier without cruelty; a victor without oppression, and a victim without murmuring."

However, the ceremony was not without incident. The next day's *Montgomery Advertiser* reported,

> More than a dozen persons were hurt, none of them seriously, yesterday afternoon at Capitol Heights when the platform used to accommodate celebrants and participants in the unveiling of a statue of Robert E. Lee collapsed. The collapse of the platform might well have caused many deaths except that it subsided gradually and its occupants were comparatively calm.
>
> The panic was slight and there was practically no injury from stampeding . . . According to the reports of those who were on or near the stage, it was the right end of the stage that first gave way. It subsided just after three veterans had stepped forward to unveil the statue of General Lee. . . . Finally with a weakening on the right the entire platform tottered forward and downward and slowly came to the earth. . . . And in the meantime,

far, far, below the debris, someone was plaintively murmuring; 'Brandy! Water! Air! Preferably brandy!"

Later, probably in the early 1950s, to open up another street off Madison Avenue, the statue was moved to a small triangle near the intersection of Madison Avenue and Ann Street. Photographs from that era show the statue, mounted on the smaller and current pedestal, almost directly in front of the Capitol Heights Baptist Church.

Changes in the layout of the intersection of Madison Avenue, Mt. Meigs Road, and Ann Street resulted in moving the statue to its current location in front of the school. Lee faces north in order not to turn his back on his enemy. Interestingly, Lee High School Hall of Fame inductee Leroy Pierce was the police officer who directed traffic associated with the move. The unveiling ceremony for the statue on the Lee campus was held May 2, 1960, with Student Council President Jim Vickrey presiding, the USMC color guard raising the flag, and the Lee High School band, directed by John Long,

In 1960, the statue was moved again to its present location in front of the school, parallel to Ann Street.

playing the national anthem. Then Lee chaplain Rev. Louis Armstrong gave the invocation, Mayor Earl James gave the dedication speech, and Miss Lee High School Mary Ellen Dendy unveiled the statue. The band played "Dixie," and Father Joseph McArdle, pastor of St. Bede's Catholic Church, prayed the benediction.

From time to time, questions have arisen regarding ownership of the statue along with discussion as to its location should the school be discontinued as a high school or moved to a new site. Suggestions range from moving the statue to the Capitol grounds, placing it in the Archives and History Building, or allowing the Confederate Memorial Park near Clanton to secure ownership.

An argument could be made that the statue is property of the City of Montgomery, since at its 1908 dedication the mayor accepted it on the City's behalf. Newspaper reports at the time of its dedication indicated that the private developer had it constructed in Ohio as a gift to the city. It was presented to the mayor by General William Oates at its unveiling on June 12, 1908. A recent examination of documents by the City Clerk revealed no transfer of ownership. Its current location at Lee High School is on property of the Montgomery County Board of Education. The school itself cannot own property, thus an argument could also be made that the Board is the sole owner.

Over the years, the cost of repairs to the statue due to vandalism in which the sword has either been taken or damaged, along with one complete refurbishing, has been borne by the school, requiring several thousands of dollars. Recent estimates to replicate and replace the statue range from $45,000 in copper and bronze to $25,000 in aluminum.

Robert E. Lee, the Man, the General, the Educator

By Roger Stifflemire

"Do your duty in all things. You cannot do more; you should never wish to do less."

This statement by the namesake of our beloved high school reflects the essence of Robert E. Lee as an outstanding ethical and moral man, supremely accomplished military leader, and lifelong educator who ended his illustrious private and public career as a college president.

Robert E. Lee was born on January 19, 1807, in Stratford Hall, Virginia, and came to military prominence during the American Civil War. He was born into Virginia aristocracy whose extended family members included a U.S. president, a chief justice of the United States, and signers of the Declaration of Independence. His father, Colonel Henry "Light-Horse Harry" Lee, was a Princeton graduate and Revolutionary War cavalry officer and hero, winning acclaim and praise from General George Washington and becoming the only officer below the rank of general to receive the "Gold Medal," awarded for his leadership at the Battle of Paulus Hook in New Jersey, on August 19, 1779. Later, he served as governor of Virginia.

The Lees overall were a historically significant Virginia and Maryland political family, whose many prominent members are known for their accomplishments in politics and the military. The patriarch, Colonel Richard Lee I, who traced his ancestry to King Henry VIII, immigrated to Virginia in 1639 and established the family fortune in tobacco. Scions include Thomas Lee, a founder of the Ohio Company and member of the Virginia House of Burgesses; Francis Lightfoot Lee and Richard Henry Lee, signers of the Declaration of Independence; Thomas Sim Lee, Governor of Maryland; Zachary Taylor, President of the United States; and Edward Douglas White, Chief Justice of the United States. Zachary Taylor's daughter, Sarah Knox Taylor, was the first wife of Confederate President Jefferson Davis.

Ohio Company founder Thomas Lee married Hannah Harrison Ludwell; their children included a number of prominent Revolutionary War and pre-Revolution political figures. Thomas Ludwell Lee was a member of the Virginia Delegates and a major contributor to and editor of George Mason's

Virginia Declaration of Rights, a precursor to the Declaration of Independence, which was signed by his brothers Richard Henry and Francis Lightfoot. A Virginia delegate to and president of the Continental Congress under the Articles of Confederation, Richard Henry later served as a U.S. Senator under the new U.S. Constitution.

Robert E. Lee (1807–70) was probably the most famous member of the Lee family. He served not only as Confederate general but also as president of what is now Washington and Lee University, which houses the Lee Chapel, burial site of many members of the Lee family, as well as the Lee family Digital Archive. He was married to Mary Anna Randolph Custis, a granddaughter of Martha Washington, and they had seven children: sons Custis, Rooney, and Rob, and daughters Mary, Annie, Agnes and Mildred. Lee saw himself as an extension of his family's greatness and at 18 enrolled at West Point Military Academy, where he became a serious student. He completed his academic work with perfect scores in artillery, infantry and cavalry and was one of six cadets in his class to graduate without a single demerit. Lee's military reputation as a brilliant tactician and battlefield commander began to develop in 1846 while serving under General Winfield Scott in the Mexican War.

Returning to civilian life, Lee found life to be boring without significant challenge. For a period of time he managed his wife's family's plantation, which had fallen into disarray. In 1859, Lee returned to the U.S. Army and was sent to a desolate cavalry post in Texas. In October 1859, he was summoned to lead a charge against John Brown at Harper's Ferry, Virginia, quashing Brown's revolt in a single hour. That success catapulted him into the forefront to lead the Union Army should the nation go to war.

When war broke out between the states, President Abraham Lincoln called upon Robert E. Lee to command Union forces. Lee's commitment to his beloved state of Virginia was so strong that he turned down the offer from President Lincoln, resigned from the Army, and returned home. At an earlier time, the Lee family had freed all slaves and had become outspoken opponents of slavery. He had serious misgivings about joining or entering a war on the slavery issue, but when Virginia voted to secede from the nation on April 18, 1861, Lee agreed to take a leadership position with the Confederate forces. After taking control of the Army of Northern Virginia in 1862, he drove the Union Army out of Richmond in the Seven Days Battle and then gained a crucial victory at Second Manassas. But by the summer of 1864 General U.S. Grant's Union forces had established firm control of the war. On a cold, dreary day in early April 1865, General Lee told an aide, "I suppose there is nothing for me to do but go and see General Grant. And I would rather die a thousand deaths." Lee humbled himself as the war ended and said, "You see what a poor sinner I am, and how unworthy to possess what was given me; for that reason it has been take away." Nevertheless, he was eventually pardoned.

Lee returned home and to his family in April 1865 and accepted the presidency of a small college in western Virginia. From that point forward, Lee dedicated himself to building his school into a world-class institution of higher learning. Under Lee's leadership, what is now Washington and Lee University developed and grew into a major research university with graduates serving around the world.

The high school on Ann Street in Montgomery received its name in honor of a great American who put aside his generalship and became a superior educational leader. It is for this reason that those of us who attended Robert E. Lee High School and have loved it all these years must forever remember and be grateful that the namesake put down his sword, picked up his pen, and made education his purpose throughout the remainder of his life.

Robert E. Lee suffered a massive stroke in October of 1870. He died at his home, surrounded by family, on October 12, 1870.

Determination to Integrate without Major Incident, 1964–65

By Clinton Carter

In 1954, the Supreme Court of the United States issued its landmark ruling in *Brown v. Board of Education of Topeka, Kansas*, declaring that the maintenance and operation of racially segregated school systems in this country was unconstitutional for such "separate" schools were inherently "unequal" and could not be made "equal." And, while much discussion and speculation about the possible impacts of the ruling were the talk of the town, the Montgomery County Board of Education and its administrative staff, along with other local elected white leaders, soon pushed the topic further back in their collective mind. Business as usual returned to public education and schools continued to be operated totally segregated by race.

Attempts by blacks to enroll their children in all-white schools were simply rebuffed at the schoolhouse door, pursuant to procedures worked out at the beginning of each school year by school officials, instructing school principals how to meet, greet, talk with, and ultimately turn away any black students desiring to attend non-black schools. Local law enforcement was on alert everywhere in case of any disruptions resulting from the attempts at enrollment.

The first significant push to integrate Montgomery public schools began in 1955 with a letter from E. D. Nixon, chairman of the local NAACP Education Committee, petitioning the Board of Education to integrate Montgomery schools. In response, the Board took up the matter at its next meeting and then issued a policy statement:

> All citizens of the City and County are to be commended for their attitude and their spirit of understanding.
>
> Your County Board of Education has given serious consideration and much thought and study to the problems which it faces in public education in this City and County. Rapid increase in enrollment in our public schools, along with limited school facilities are conditions that

existed prior to the decision of the Supreme Court and they pose additional problems for your Board. Your County Board has been diligent in its efforts to meet the ever-increasing demand for public education of both races in our County. The new school houses erected in the City and County stand as physical evidence of our efforts to provide additional facilities of the best type possible and they have not been restricted based on race rather on the availability of finances. The need of all children of school age has been the determining factor.

Integration of our school system at this time is impossible without disrupting the entire educational system of the County. A majority of the residents of Montgomery County are opposed at this time to integration of our school system and this is a fact which we cannot ignore and was not ignored by the Supreme Court of the United States in its supplemental decision. Any attempted integration would result in substantially curtailing public education here and would hamper the efficient operation of Montgomery's public school system with the probable result of its complete disruption.

The public school system of Montgomery County must operate in accordance with the constitution and statutory law of the State of Alabama as well in accordance with the decisions of the Supreme Court of the United States.

Your Board of Education desires to promote progress in the education of the children of this County; to advance the public school system as the local conditions permit; all in accordance with the constitution and laws of the State of Alabama and the decision of the Supreme Court of the United States.

However, your Board recognizes that this can be done only through the cooperation of the citizens of this County and as our local situations justify.

Therefore, it has been decided by the Board of Education of the City and County of Montgomery as follows:

That in the interest of public education in this County, the present educational organization shall remain in force.

That the Board of Education of the City and County of Montgomery shall make or cause to be made a study of the question of integration in our public schools to determine if such is practicable and possible; if so, how, when and to what extent integration can be accomplished.

That pending this study, and in order to promote public education in the County, consideration be given to the operation of the Alabama Placement Act of 1955, together with the constitutional and statutory law of Alabama and the decisions of the Supreme Court of the United States.

That this Board does not intend to defy or ignore the lawful authority and decisions of the United States and the State of Alabama. This Board takes cognizance of local conditions and situations and will do all in our power to achieve the best possible results in the field public education for both races. We will take no hasty action that may work to the detriment of the education of the youth of this County. We will take whatever action may be necessary to avoid disruption of our entire public school system."

So it was not until May 11, 1964—a decade after *Brown*—that civil rights attorney Fred Gray sued the Montgomery County Board of Education in federal court in *Carr v. Montgomery County Board of Education*. Gray asked for an injunction to stop the Board from continuing a compulsory biracial public school system and from assigning students, teachers, and other school personnel on the basis of race. (Arlam Carr Jr., the plaintiff, became one of the first black students to integrate Lanier High School in the fall of 1964, and went on to have a career at WSFA-TV before he died in 2014.)

District Judge Frank M. Johnson Jr. presided over the trial of the case in the federal courthouse now named for him in Montgomery.

On July 31, 1964, Judge Johnson certified the plaintiffs as a class under the Rules of Civil Procedure, and he noted that the one school district for Montgomery County was under the complete control of the Board and superintendent, with an enrollment in the school year 1963–64 of 15,000 black children and 25,000 white children, attending 77 schools.

He found that the Montgomery County Board of Education operated a dual system based upon race and color, with principals, teachers and other professional personnel assigned to schools in accordance with the race of the students and with transportation designed to transport students to schools of their own race.

Exhibits in the case indicated that attendance areas were designed to segregate students by race, including the "feeder system," and that race played a role in the expenditure of school funds for maintenance, operation, and construction in the school system.

Another finding of the Court was that the Alabama School Placement Act (enacted in 1955 in hopes of avoiding the requirements of *Brown*) had not resulted in a transfer of any black students to white schools or of any white students to black schools, and thus the Board continued to operate a dual system based on race and had taken no positive steps to desegregate its schools.

Judge Johnson thus concluded that there was no lawful justification for continuing a segregated school system, and he restrained the Board and the superintendent from continuing such a system. He ordered that with the beginning of the 1964–65 school year, the first, tenth, eleventh and twelfth grades were to be desegregated by application of the Alabama School Placement Law after advertisement in the newspaper, such applications to be accepted until August 14, 1964.

The Board was further ordered to file by January 15, 1965, a plan effective with the 1965–66 school year that would desegregate the entire school system. Due to delays caused by appeals and motions by both plaintiffs and defendants, the plan was not implemented as scheduled. By the start of the 1965 school term, only a few additional black students had joined those who had enrolled in formerly all-white schools the previous fall.

Second Major Court Order

On March 22, 1966, Judge Johnson showed his impatience with the minimal progress being made to desegregate the school system. His orders became much more specific regarding what was required of the Board and to prove documentation of their efforts. The Board was ordered to execute a plan for complete desegregation and to make annual reports with racial breakdowns on enrollment and assignment of professional personnel to each school. All grades except 5 and 6 were ordered to be desegregated under a freedom of choice basis commencing with the school term in September 1966. Grades 5 and 6 were to be desegregated in September 1977.

Freedom of Choice Plan

A part of the March 22 Order concerned "freedom of choice." Under freedom of choice, exercised annually, any student, black or white, could elect to attend a school in which his/her race was in the minority. The concern that school officials might attempt to sway students from electing enrollment under the freedom of choice option led Judge Johnson to order officials not to interfere with the enrollment process.

Students electing enrollment under freedom of choice could be denied only for reasons of overcrowding at the school they chose. Rules and timelines were established for the application procedure. A review of the various stipulations regarding applications reveal a number of weaknesses that allowed some school officials to "work the system" to reduce the number of applications. It was not unusual for some forms to become "misplaced" or rejected on technicalities. And the fact that forms were to be returned to the superintendent's office and not to the schools, although designed to reduce the chance of manipulation or mismanagement, no doubt discouraged some who wished to apply. In any case, I do not recall hearing of any significant issues with the process.

Transportation services were required to make major changes in operation. The order required students electing a school under freedom of choice to receive transportation to that school if the distance from the school met the two-mile requirement for transportation services afforded all other students in the system. It was not unusual to see small numbers of students on buses being delivered to schools because of this change and more and more buses were making multiple runs before and after school each day.

The order made clear that every student would have full access to all services, activities, and programs (including transportation, athletics, and other extra curricular activities). Waiting periods and transfer rules for athletics, including those prescribed by the Alabama Athletic Association, were disallowed.

Faculty and Staff

In a later order, Judge Johnson imposed a ratio regarding assignment of teachers and professional staff, however, his March 22, 1966, order did not go that far, apparently again giving the Board an opportunity to make progress on this issue. It simply ordered the Board to cease assigning personnel to schools where their race mirrored the race of the students. It gave the Board an opportunity to desegregate faculties by encouraging transfers. It gave the Board an opportunity to desegregate faculties by assigning new hires to schools without regard to race, and it prohibited the Board from dismissing, demoting, or rehiring personnel on the basis of race.

Closing of Inadequate Facilities

At the time of the 1966 order, a number of schools were closed. First, those closed were small, enrolled only black students, and were in generally deplorable condition. Students were taught in the "combination class" style of the day in an environment where the only teaching aids were a chalkboard and a small allotment of chalk provided by the school system. Books, if any, were old, tattered and out-of-date. I believe I am correct in stating that none had indoor restroom or lunchroom facilities. These schools, because of their size, did not have principals as we know them today. One teacher was designated to be in charge as "principal teacher" and the designation of "principal" evolved from that designation.

Seven elementary schools were ordered closed effective with the 1966–67 school year. They were: Abraham's Vineyard; Phillips; Cecil; Arthur Cook; Battle; McCant's, and Kate Bowen.

Fourteen schools were ordered closed effective with the 1967–68 school year. They were: Alice White, Arrington, Big Zion, Tankersley, Chappell Gray, G. W. Trenholm, Lillian Dungee, Waugh, Woodley, Zion Hill, McLean, McLemore, Lillian Dabney, and Zion Road.

The Third Order

In February 1968, the Board once again found itself in Judge Johnson's courtroom, resulting in yet further and still more specific orders on August 1, 1968, regarding the elimination of the dual school system.

After reviewing previous orders, the Court made several observations. It noted that approximately 550 black students were attending traditionally white schools whereas no white children were attending traditionally black schools. As of February 1968, only 32 classroom teachers were assigned to schools of the other race while there were 550 black teachers and 815 white teachers in the system. Practically all new hires in the system continued to be assigned schools where their race mirrored the student body and no progress had been made in the use of substitute teachers to desegregate. White substitutes simply refused to work in traditionally black schools. Night school faculties continued to be completely segregated.

The Court also noted that athletic contests continued to be restricted to play on a racially divided basis. White schools competed with other white schools and black schools competed with other black schools. At that time there were two athletic associations—one for white schools and one for black schools. Association rules prevented cross-competition.

Judge Johnson was sharply critical in his finding that the Board had continued to construct new schools and to add to others in an attempt to keep the races separate. The new Jefferson Davis High School, the Peter Crump Elementary School and the Southlawn Elementary School had been constructed in a size that would accommodate the immediate white neighborhoods, no doubt to attempt to limit enrollment of black students by applying the overcrowding feature of the freedom of choice option. To further raise the ire of the Court, the Board had declared these schools as to be "non-transported" zones, again attempting to eliminate enrollment of black students who would have otherwise been eligible to ride the bus. The Court also considered "aggravating" the Board's decision to give a school a name (Jefferson Davis) and to allow the design of a crest for that school that both signaled that the school was for whites only. It did not help the Board's position when Jefferson Davis opened with a white principal, a white band director, and three white coaches, and had engaged in fund-raising activities only in the white community. Remedy for the elimination of segregated athletic contests was reserved until another case (*Lee v. Macon*) had been heard and a ruling made.

The Board was put on notice that if the freedom of choice plan continued to have little impact on changes in the racial composition of traditionally white schools, other means would be put in place. It was at this point in the Order that the Court became even more specific on what was required of the Board:

FACULTY AND STAFF. The Board was required to desegregate faculty so that in each school the ratio of white to black teachers would be substantially the same as the then present composition of teachers employed in the system which constituted a ratio of 3 whites to 2 blacks. The accomplishment of this Order had to be done by inducing volunteers and then by filing vacancies and transfers.

SUBSTITUTE TEACHERS. The ratio of the number of days taught by white substitute teachers to the number of days taught by black substitutes will reflect the ratio of white substitutes to black substitutes on the list. No substitute could specify an assignment so as to restrict himself/herself to schools reflecting their own race.

STUDENT TEACHERS. The same ratio used by substitutes also applied to student teachers.

NIGHT SCHOOLS. The same ratio as that stated for Faculty and Staff above.

NEW CONSTRUCTION. Approval from the State Superintendent required with the intent of not allowing construction if it perpetuated the dual school system.

TRANSPORTATION. Cease operating overlapping and duplicative routes based on race.

JEFFERSON DAVIS HIGH SCHOOL. The choices of black students electing to attend would be honored.

COMPLIMENTING THE BOARD

In another Order regarding desegregation requirements issued on August 1, 1968 the Board had challenged the fixed mathematical ration impose with regard to teacher assignments. The challenge was rejected. However, the Court commented that "Some five times during the period from 1964 to 1967, the district court publicly complimented the Montgomery County School Board on its efforts toward achieving desegregation," and ". . . when it is compared with some other similar operations is a considerable feat, for which this community, in my judgment, owes these school officials their appreciation. It evidences a pattern of professional conduct that other systems could, for the benefit of their students, emulate." Despite the accolades, the fixed mathematical ratio was affirmed after appeal by the Board.

LEE'S FIRST BLACK STUDENTS

At Lee High School, the first black students enrolled at the beginning of the 1964–65 school year were Willie Riggins Jr., his sister, Annie Joyce (Riggins) Williams, and Julia Sanders. They reported for classes a few days after school started in 1964, local leaders anticipating racial unrest that did not occur. FBI agents accompanied these students for several days, taking them early from each of their classes so as to avoid mingling with the student body during class changes. The first assembly held in the new auditorium was for the purpose of informing the student body that these students would be arriving and to instill a sense of calm for the implementation of this historic event. A few other African American students were also enrolled in other Montgomery Public Schools at the beginning of the 1964–65 school year.

Following their enrollment in 1964, only five black students were pictured in the 1968–69 yearbook, increasing to the forty-one pictured in the 1969–70 yearbook, all attending under the Freedom of Choice option. One barrier to further enrollment of black students was that no transportation was provided those who elected to enroll under this plan.

Eventually, the federal court was petitioned to take additional action to insure substantial integration, and Judge Frank M. Johnson ordered the Montgomery County Board of Education to establish attendance zones and to close a number of schools, including Booker T. Washington High School, at the end of the 1969–70 school year. That order required transportation for all students who met the distance requirement that had been long established for other students.

With the opening of the 1970–71 school year, Lee High and Jefferson Davis High received a majority of the Booker T. Washington High students. The 1970–71 yearbook depicts 169 black students, approximately 7 percent of the student body.

The first black faculty member to teach at Lee was Mrs. Louise Spears in the Business Education Department. Mrs. Spears, now deceased, was the sister-in-law of Mr. Henry Spears, the first black member and eventually president of the Montgomery County Board of Education.

As I researched and wrote the above, it was a satisfying experience to locate, interview, and receive comments from the three pioneering students. Each has written below, exclusively for this book, about their experiences in preparing for, enrolling in, and completing the 1964–65 school year at Lee High School. Willie and Julia were graduated in 1965; Joyce was awarded her diploma the following year.

I also want to note that Mr. E. D. Nixon, who first sought to desegregate Montgomery's schools in 1955, continued his efforts on behalf of black children in Montgomery, maintaining close ties with central office administrators (particularly with his close friend and ally, Associate Superintendent Thomas Bobo) and working with them to further his goals. In recognition of his persistence and influence, the Montgomery County Board of Education, on my recommendation while I served as Superintendent of Education, named a new elementary school on Goode Street in his honor. Later, the Montgomery City Council changed the name of the street on which the school is located to E. D. Nixon Avenue.

My Lee Experience

By Willie Riggins Jr.

My involvement began during the summer of 1964. While participating in a Freedom March Rally, I was inspired enough to believe that I could integrate the public school system. I, my sister Joyce Riggins and a friend, Julia Sanders, decided that we could and should volunteer to be amongst the first to integrate the public school system at the high school level.

We were able to ride the existing wave of support for any form of integration. Initially, my family was apprehensive and nervous, but they were resolved to support us with this endeavor. We received similar support from the community. The only major concern I had was for my safety, but those concerns were abated on the first day.

Three weeks before the beginning of school, I was notified by a registered letter from Montgomery Public Schools that I had been accepted as a student at Robert E. Lee High School. The Montgomery Improvement Association, led by Fred Gray and Johnnie Carr, arranged for a federal security detail to escort us to school. The security personnel ensured our safety by clearing the streets and surrounding areas outside of the school. In addition, they cleared the hallways within the school before our arrival. As such, we were not subjected to the demeaning abuse that is traditionally associated with an event of this nature. With the help of drivers who volunteered to take us to and from school, our safety was assured.

On the first day, the campus was completely clear of all distractions. There were no protestors outside the campus nor were there any students roaming the halls. I was escorted to class by security. The students and teachers were expecting me. I was greeted by name and in each class I was assigned the first seat in the first row. I did not exchange classes with the other students. I waited until all students were in their classes and seated before moving to my next class. However, as concerns dissipated, I was able to move with the other students.

Primarily, the students reacted by "not" reacting. Other than staring, there were no overt gestures of protest or support. On occasion I would be acknowledged with a head nod, but I was generally left alone. I expected and was generally prepared for much harsher treatment, but no such treatment ever occurred. There was only one incident in which I involved the administration. While coming up the stairs, a student threw a piece of gum that landed on my sweater. Initially, I chased him, but I immediately stopped and reported the incident to a teacher. I was referred to the office where I met with Mr. Clinton Carter, the assistant principal. Although he was empathetic, he was stern with his advice. He advised me to keep my composure, because I was an agent of change. I was establishing a precedent and setting an example that could not tolerate any negativity. I heeded his advice and allowed the incident to pass.

It is my belief that the students were prepared for my arrival. The civil rights movement was active and receiving national attention. The Freedom Riders were active and receiving national attention. The violence and abuse associated with the civil rights movement had been receiving national attention. The federal government had been applying a significant amount of pressure on local governments to desegregate. The integration of the public schools system seemed more like a natural progression than a violation. This probably minimized the propensity for incidents that would have been caused by the surprise or shock of my presence.

My school day was about as normal as could be expected. There were no particular incidents of which to speak. I ate lunch daily in the cafeteria with my sister and Julia. On occasion, students would acknowledge their acceptance with a head nod or wink of the eye, but there were never any overt gestures of acceptance or rejection. I was not allowed to participate in any extracurricular activities. I attempted to play football, but I was told that the risks were "too high" and my safety could not be assured.

By spring, the novelty of my presence had begun to wear off. Students would openly greet me and engage in minimal conversation. I was able to move about more freely, but I was still barred from participation in extracurricular activities. The continued ban was easily the worst part of the entire experience. As a senior, I was hopeful that I would have an active and memorable year. Although this didn't happen, I accepted my role and was satisfied with the decision.

At the end of the year, I bought a yearbook. Surprisingly, several students asked to sign my yearbook and I was asked to sign theirs. My brother, a teacher at South Macon, took the yearbook to his class and used it as a teaching tool to illustrate the changes occurring in society. Being a representative of such change was the best part of the experience. The public school system was one of the final barriers to be broken. The integration of the public school system was necessary to close the gap caused by segregation. Although I was denied participation in extracurricular activities, I was afforded a quality education and a level of exposure that I could not have otherwise received.

My Lee Experience

By Annie Joyce (Riggins) Williams

I attended Robert E. Lee High School for two years, 1964–65 and 1965–66. I got to attend Lee because a group of leaders of the NAACP and supporters of Dr. Martin Luther King approached my parents about my brother and me enrolling there. We were chosen because we lived within walking distance of the school and they felt school segregation should be abolished. My parents said yes and our journey began. I was in the eleventh grade. We were given a series of placement tests by the board of education. As it turned out, we had taken courses in the previous grades that were being offered in our present grade at Lee and substitute courses were given. We were assigned to a reliable person to drive us to and from school each day followed by federal security.

We encountered a lot of yelling and obscenity along the way which made it very uncomfortable upon arrival at school. Mrs. Goodwin was my homeroom teacher and I found her to be kind and professional. In her classroom and in every classroom, we were always put in the first desk by the door and pulled up and away from the other classmates. Whether it was for our safety or not, segregation still existed. Mrs. Clements (Typing), Mrs. Grissette (Home Ec.), and Mr. Grover Jacobs (Law) were excellent teachers. I was very comfortable in their classrooms. They gave me help when I needed it and treated me like all the other students. I also remember Ms. Nichols—she wasn't my teacher, she was Willie's teacher, but I liked her very much—she was a very nice person and it showed.

For every one or two kids that were nice, a dozen or more were extremely cruel which made it difficult to concentrate on class work. I remember ruining one of my nice dresses when someone put gum in my chair when I returned to my seat after going to the bathroom. We were harassed at home via phone calls; my dad lost his job and my mother lost one of hers (she did domestic work and my father worked at Empire Rouse Laundry).

I think it was a very positive thing that I enrolled, attended and graduated from Robert E. Lee High School. I got the opportunity to take courses like typing, law, home economics, and business math which I never would have from my previous school. I became a good seamstress (my mom says it's in my genes). I learned to appreciate my parents, family and how to interact with people outside my race. You don't have to like everyone, just be courteous and show respect.

After graduating from Lee in 1966, I started college at Alabama State University. I was there for two years, then got married and moved to Philadelphia, Pennsylvania. I worked 20 years for a book publishing division of CBS network. During those years I had two children, Courtney (son) and Stacey (daughter); enrolled at LaSalle University where I graduated with a BA degree in English in 1986. In later years, I worked for US Healthcare/Aetna where I became a supervisor of administration and managed 22-plus people until I retired in 2010. I am now a widow and continue to live in Philadelphia.

My Lee Experience

By Julia Sanders

I was one of the first three African American students to enroll at Robert E. Lee High School in the fall of 1964 under the Freedom of Choice option that had been ordered by the federal court. Before enrolling at Lee, I attended Booker T. Washington High School.

My parents and I, as well as other families in my neighborhood, were visited by civil rights recruiters to encourage us to transfer to Robert E. Lee High School, which was in close proximity. I was quite willing to make the transfer, because I saw an opportunity to enhance and expand my educational learning with access to more and better tools and resources. I did so without any fear. And, Lee High School was, indeed, adequately equipped for productive learning. In fact, I was amazed in comparison to Booker T.

Washington and its very limited equipment and resources. I can remember thinking: why could they not have better equipped the black schools to provide an environment conducive to education before integrating?

On the first day of school, we wore sunglasses in an effort to shield our identity from the media and onlookers. We were transported to and from school by several cooperative adults during the entire school year.

With the exceptions of two, I did not feel rejected by my teachers or administrators. I did not sense resentment or bias from them. I felt comfortable in their classroom. So I would say my classroom experiences with these individuals were positive. Also, at one point during the school year, a threat to engage me in a fight was made by a white boy. I was surprised to learn that several students had made reports to the office regarding this student. I was also informed by the school administrators that they had dealt with him and that I had nothing to fear from him. This positive support was a relief.

There were many fellow students that were friendly and supportive. I was convinced that more students wanted to get to know us but were afraid of repercussions. In fact, it happened in one of my classes, not only from several of the students but the teacher also. There were sneers and negative body language toward this student. This particular teacher also erroneously marked my assignments and tests and would not look or listen when I tried to discuss the matter. In fact, she deliberately flunked me in her course and caused me to enroll in summer school to finish my senior year. The course was shorthand. I was an "A" student in shorthand. In fact, I knew I was good. I later regretted not pursuing the matter.

I personally had no problem with the seating arrangements in the classroom. However, I did not like being isolated in the lunchroom the entire school year. I understood that it was to prevent racial tension, but felt it was poor judgment being placed by the windows where those with biased feelings could point and make racial comments while we were having lunch.

I personally felt that we were not asked to participate in extracurricular activities because the school environment was not prepared to accommodate, especially with this being the first year of high school integration in Montgomery, Alabama.

I am thankful for the positive learning experiences that I received at

Robert E. Lee. I did not place blame on those who exhibited bias because I was intelligent enough to know that they were the product of a background in race relations that made it difficult to adjust and/or accept.

Following graduation, I sought employment in the Montgomery area. Dealing with the fact of discrimination in employment was far more traumatic than integration of a school. I finally decided to move to Detroit to seek employment. I worked for a couple of years with AAA Insurance Company before moving back home. It took some time, but I eventually became employed with the State of Alabama and retired in December 2010 with 40-plus years of service.

6

Stars Fell on Lee High School

By Clinton Carter

The First Faculty and Staff

The total administrative/supervisory staff when Robert E. Lee High School opened in the fall of 1955 consisted of the principal, one acting assistant principal, a lunchroom manager, and a dean of girls/director of activities.

As noted in chapter four, the faculty consisted of 35 highly qualified and effective professionals. Among those were:

Miss Gladys Nichols, a revered teacher of English who served as a military hostess for the Army during WWII; Mrs. Margaret Weldon, also an English teacher who often chided restless students by accusing them of making "rat noises"; and Mr. J. L. Price, physics teacher who was a good teacher, but rough-hewn and was known when teaching the principle of the lever to refer to it as a "pry pole" and for teaching the ups and downs of what he uniquely referred to as "Pacific gravity."

Mr. Russell Berry, a great student of history, as evident in his teaching, was in the U.S. Army Reserve and later became a two-star general. Coach Tom Jones, head football coach and math teacher, arrived at the school before 5 a.m. from his home in Lowndes County. Mr. Guy Medley, teacher of industrial arts (woodworking), had a reputation for throwing objects at unruly students and once threw a large wrench at a student, barely missing his head; the wrench broke a window in the shop before landing outside.

Band Director Johnny Long will go down in history as a great musician and motivator; among other things he was adept at having the band play loudly when opposing football teams were in their huddle, thus creating what we called the "Johnny Long Defense." Assistant football coach Jim Chafin, a great role model, would succeed Tom Jones as head coach and go on to win state championships in 1969 and 1970. Fred Guy and James Bozeman, both great teachers of math, later became Lee principals. Helen Blackshear, teacher of English and a poet and author, became Poet Laureate of Alabama. Activities Director Annie Laurie Lindsey wrote Lee's "Alma Mater."

Early on, Lee students recognized that the teaching they were being offered at their brand new school was no "lost tradition." Indeed, during the very first year, 1955–56, students recognized a number of outstanding teachers in the *Stars and Bars*.

The first "Teacher of the Week" selected was Miss Sarah Johnson, who taught art and history. Holding the B.S. degree from Troy State Teachers College and the M.S. from the University of Alabama and having done graduate work at George Peabody College for Teachers in Nashville, she was a member of the American Association of University Women and vice president of the Department of Art Education of the Alabama Education Association, as well as one of the sponsors of the Senior Class.

The second honoree was Mr. Russell Berry, American history and English teacher, who had served in World War II and had a second term of active duty service in the Army before beginning his teaching career in Yatesville, Georgia, then moving to Montgomery's new high school. He had a B.S. from Auburn and taught all aspects of history, including civics and geography. While he was considered "hard," he was unusually popular with students, eventually serving as one of two sponsors of the Senior Class, the teacher representative to Youth Legislature, and chairman of the Faculty Advisory Committee. Nell Rushton McGilberry ('57), remembers him fondly as a wonderful teacher in whose classes students wanted to be. In fact, some took American History in summer school to be sure they got him, for only he taught the course then, she reports. Mr. Berry had a partial hearing loss, a souvenir of WWII, and was eligible for disability benefits, she recalls, but he told his students that his country owed him nothing and he owed

Russell Berry   *Gladys Nichols*

his country everything—a lesson that has stayed with his other students through the years, as he advanced through the U.S. Army Reserve to the rank of two-star general. Jim Vickrey ('60) remembers Mr. Berry using a golf club Johnny Carson-style as a prop while lecturing "and occasionally to get the attention of a wayward-leaning student." Even after he had left Lee to begin a new career at the State Department of Education, he remained interested in Lee High School, serving in 1994 as the initial chair of the Hall of Fame Committee then as co-chair with Vickrey.

The next "Teacher of the Week" that first year was Mr. P. L. Woodham, who taught math. He received his undergraduate and master's degrees from the University of Alabama. Before coming to Lee, Mr. Woodham taught and served as a junior high school principal in Geneva County and taught at Lanier High School. His three years in the Army during WWII included twelve months in the Pacific Theatre.

English teacher Charles Cox was the fourth Lee teacher to be honored by the school paper and no doubt the tallest. He had served four years in the U.S. Marine Corps, including two years with the 1st Marine Division in the Pacific. His experiences during a Guadalcanal skirmish made him a war hero who was featured in a book. He earned both his B.S. and M.S.

degrees from Auburn.

Another teacher honored that first year was Miss Gladys Nichols, one of Lee High's most feared but beloved teachers of English. A B.S. and M.A. graduate of the University of Alabama, she taught at Montgomery County High School and served as Rural Recreation Director for Pike and Dale Counties. During WWII, she was an Army hostess and later served as an auditor for Army Finance in Chicago and St. Louis. The students of Baldwin County High School dedicated their yearbook to Miss Nichols and at Lee she served as sponsor of the Junior Class.

Next was Mr. Elmore Hall, who also taught English and helped his share of Lee graduates to survive collegiate studies in his field before he himself "graduated" to the Extension Course Institute at Gunter AFB where he edited textbooks for the USAF's world-wide correspondence school. During WWII, he served in the Navy, seeing action in the Pacific. After his discharge, he attended Huntingdon College and received his B.A. in English and history from Auburn, then did his graduate work at the University of Alabama. His hobby was reported to be raising Tennessee walking horses and writing poetry, some of which was published.

Mrs. Sue Sandusky was honored as Teacher of the Week on May 4, 1956. A Troy State Teachers College graduate (B.S.), she taught physical education and math in Marianna prior to coming to Lee. At Lee, she taught physical education and history.

Featured in the *Stars and Bars* of May 18, 1956, was Mrs. Marcella Foster, head of Lee's Commercial Department. She was a Lanier High graduate and earned her B.S. at the University of Alabama and her M.S. at Auburn.

Miss Ellyn Dudley was featured because of her splendid work as the choral director in Lee's outstanding music program. She also graduated from Lanier and received her B.S. from Troy State Teachers College. At Lee, her choral groups won numerous "superior" awards in choral competitions across the state.

In the final edition of the *Stars and Bars* for 1955–56, Mr. L. L. Boone and Mrs. Eunice Day were recognized. Mr. Boone played football and baseball at Valley High School in Fairfax before being drafted into the Navy for six years. He served in the Atlantic and Pacific theatres. He received

L. L. Boone

his B.S. from Livingston State Teachers College and a master's in school administration from Peabody College in Nashville. He then taught at Covington County High in Florala and Cullman High before coming to Lee. Mrs. Day was Lee High's long-time Latin teacher. She did her collegiate work at Tift College and the University of Georgia. She told the newspaper that she especially liked to work with teenagers and felt that helping young people make decisions was a very important job, since students have so many problems to solve during their high school years. Among those problems for some of her students were such challenges as memorizing the Lord's Prayer in Latin and trying to read Caesar and Cicero in their original language, experiences many, especially those who became lawyers and doctors, still trade on.

APPEARING IN THE AWARD-WINNING 1956 yearbook were Principal Tim Carlton and Acting Assistant Principal L. L. (Lee) Boone, who later served as the first Lee vice principal and then as principal of Capitol Heights Junior School. In addition to his duties as acting assistant principal, he taught history and geography and served as sponsor of Lee Hi-Y and the "Nut Club."

Other teachers and staff members pictured in the 1956 yearbook and their subject matters were Addie Adourian, math and sponsor of the sophomore class; Marjorie Bagwell, commercial subjects, including touch-typing; Dr. Joanna Breedlove, French and history and French Club sponsor; Coach James R. ("Jim") Chafin, science and athletics; M. T. Duncan, diversified occupations and sponsor of the junior class; Frances Fuller, commercial subjects;

Josephine Grissette, home economics and sponsor of the Home Economics Club and cheerleaders; Jo Hodge, Spanish and English and sponsor of the Spanish Club and later the school's first counselor; Dorothy Holley, commercial subjects and sponsor of Gamma Tri-Hi-Y; Corrie King, English, and a *Scabbard* sponsor; Jean McCurdy, biology; Head Football Coach Tom Jones, math and athletics and sponsor of the "L" Club; John Long, director of the award-winning, trend-setting marching band program; Guy Medley, mechanical drawing and manual arts; J. L. Price, chemistry and physics and sponsor of the Physics Club, who never met a wide tie or a student group he didn't like; Dorothea Putnam, commercial subjects; Anacile Riggs, distributive education; Faye Sessions, commercial subjects and sponsor of the "Nut Club"; Mary Smith, biology and Hi-Y sponsor; Charlotte Speight, math and sponsor of Zeta Tri-Hi-Y and Lee Hi-Y; Ann Thompson, English and dramatics and sponsor of Rebel Tri-Hi-Y and the Dramatics Club; Mattie Bell Cook, lunchroom manager, who created the Principal's Dining Room out of one of her pantries; George Peters, former shop teacher at Capitol Heights Junior High School and Lee coach, who accompanied some of his students to Lee; and Louise Smyth, school secretary.

Josephine Grissette

On August 4, 2014, Mrs. Josephine Grissette—at the time, 96, still living alone and driving herself to and from church, the grocery store, and her doctors' offices—gave a delightful interview to this author, recounting her early years at Lee. She recalled that she came to Lee from Capitol Heights Junior High, along with teachers Mayme Danley and Marcella Foster, lunchroom manager Mattie Bell Cook, and secretary Louise Smyth. She remembered that before the first day of the first year that Lee High School opened, Mr. Carlton asked her to provide refreshments for the incoming staff. The resulting reception was followed by a tour of the new physical plant.

The Kind of Students Lee Teachers Taught

Although it is generally understood and appreciated that students at Lee during the first decade were exceptionally motivated to learn and succeed, little data can be retrieved to support this observation. The cumulative record cards of students are subject to privacy laws and cannot be accessed without approval of the individual. Thus the door is closed to that source of information, as well as to student registers, if any still exist, kept by teachers in which basic biographical data, such as home addresses, names and occupations of parents or guardians and daily attendance records, were kept. Fortunately for a number of former students, no disciplinary records were kept after they were graduated or otherwise left Lee.

What constituted the highly motivated student body? First, most students came from homes whose parents were engaged in what is commonly known as blue-collar occupations, including work at industries such as Brockway Glass and a cotton mill, both located in the Chishom/Boylston area. Many were salespersons, including those at automobile dealerships, insurance agencies, and general clothing and merchandise stores, including Montgomery Fair, Belk's, and others. Some worked as mechanics, drivers for the city bus line, and for the maintenance department of the City of

Lee students were from blue-collar backgrounds with supportive parents.

Donald Davis

Montgomery. A few owned their businesses, but for the most part parents worked for others. Most mothers did not work outside the home.

Most homes in the Lee area were small by today's standards, attesting to the modest incomes of parents. Family automobiles—rarely more than one per household—were more functional than flashy, reflecting the no-nonsense approach to life and reinforcing the value of hard work in the formational years of Lee students. Those enjoying the greatest academic success as well as future success across a spectrum of occupations included those from what we today would consider poor. Donald Davis ('58, HOF 2004), a resident of the Chisholm community, remembers that upon his enrollment at Lee he entered a zone of culture shock. His mother, using her budget checks from Montgomery Fair, rode with Donald to the Fair to "dress him up" for high school. She was an excellent seamstress, but he insisted that he would not wear a homemade shirt on the first school day. He recalled riding the bus "from across the tracks" through Highland Gardens into Capitol Heights, seeing homes that were new and brick, whereas he remembers only two brick homes in Chisholm at the time. Donald says, "I never had a mediocre teacher. I often wonder how they put together such an outstanding faculty at a new school. The football team and band had a culture all their own. They cared for their people." Donald's preparation at Lee prepared him for success in college and in his career where he retired as a vice president of Kraft Foods. His is one of the many stories of successful Lee students who can point back to their experiences at Lee and credit excellent, supporting faculty who prepared them for life's challenges.

What then contributed to student success? The fact that most students came from homes where both parents were present most of the time and who cared about and carefully watched the progress of their children was a major factor. Parents were involved in all activities of the school, from the PTA to the band, athletics, and other extra-curricular activities. They had confidence in the school's administrators and teachers and afforded them respect. This was ingrained in their children who also respected their teachers. Parents simply wanted their children to have the knowledge and skills necessary to do better in life than they themselves had done. Perhaps this is the key, for students also had the same goal.

Religion and religious activities played a major role in the lives of parents and students. They attended and were involved in church activities, learning biblical truths that helped them gain appreciation for the value in helping others and in forming healthy relationships that have lasted a lifetime. Religious discipline, especially Bible studies, thus helped many a Lee student to apply him/herself to the subject of other subjects, and to hold in high regard those teaching them how.

Stars Generated by Stars

Perhaps the best indicator, and at least the one verifiable by public information, is the success of Lee students who competed for scholarships

Student-led prayer during the lunch period. Faith was important to most Lee students, and it was the theme of the 1957 Scabbard.

through the National Merit Scholarship Program. This program was established in 1955, according to the NMSP's website, "at a time in which there was concern that the United States was lagging behind in the cold war scientific race, but the public was indifferent to rewarding intellectual accomplishment. In response the National Merit Scholarship Program was founded to identify and honor scholastically talented American youth and to encourage them to develop their abilities to the fullest."

In 1956, there were 59,158 entrants from 10,388 participating high schools. By 1965 there were 806,991 entrants from 17,162 participating high schools. The 1956 *Scabbard* does not picture any NMSP entrants. Since the test is given in October each year, one might speculate that no Lee students became entrants, having entered Lee just one month before.

The 1957 *Scabbard* pictured Barbara Shell, Carolyn Saari, David Cannon, and Angeline Waites as National Merit finalists.

The 1958 *Scabbard* did not include names or photos of NSMCP entrants. Information could not be found to support whether the yearbook simply decided to omit this as a feature or whether there were no entrants for the 1957–58 school years.

SEMI-FINALISTS, NATIONAL MERIT SCHOLARSHIP EXAMINATION

Runners-up to the semi-finalists in the National Merit Scholarship Examination are: FIRST ROW: Carolyn Taylor, Virginia zer, Nell Rushton, Annette Kennedy . . . SECOND ROW: Laurence Peirce, Dick Bond . . . NOT PICTURED: Bonnie Pitts and Luther Crabb.

Many Lee students, like these semi-finalists from 1958–59, were honored through the National Merit program during the school's first decade.

Beginning with the 1958–59 school year, the *Scabbard* began recognizing students who had earned all "A's" for three consecutive years along with NMSP finalists and runners-up. Recognized for earning all "A's" were: Dale Martin, Carol Muse, Patricia Morgan, Shirley McGuff, and Carolyn Taylor. Recognized as National Merit Semi-Finalists were: Judy Brantley, Karen King, Tad Bowman, and Carol Muse. Carolyn Taylor, Virginia Inzer, Nell Rushton, Annette Kennedy, Laurence Pierce, Dick Bond, Luther Crabb, and Bonnie Pitts were recognized as National Merit runners-up.

The 1960 *Scabbard* included names and photos of those earning all "A's" for three years and of those who were National Merit Finalists. Earning all "A's" were" Kent Williams, Dianne Sharits, Richard Snaider, Bonnie Brice, and Mickey Jenkins. National Merit Finalists were Bonnie Brice, Tom Fisher, Mickey Jenkins, Jean Frandenburg, Tom Borden, Carolyn Price, Jim Hall, Diane Sharits, and Kent Williams.

The 1961 *Scabbard* recognized Worth Whiteside and Thomas Norwood for having earned all "A's" for three consecutive years. Randy Hall, Wayne Scott, Horace McWhorter, Jerry Lide, Leonard Lampkin, Steve Kocial, Zane Hoit, and Thomas Norwood were recognized as National Merit Semi-Finalists.

The 1962 *Scabbard* recognized Terry Smith, Marion Marsh, and Betty Willis for having earned all "A's" for three consecutive years. Mike Tuley,

Lee students working diligently in a typical classroom scene during the first decade.

Marion Marsh, Kathleen Maloney, Pat Flanagan, Douglas Birkhead, and David Pettus were recognized as National Merit Finalists.

The 1963 *Scabbard* recognized Walter Horn, Martha Huey, Joan Hartley, Kitty Dean, Carolyn Johnson, Jane Anderson and Martha Myers for having earned all "A's" for three consecutive years. Joan Hartley, Jane Anderson, John Ellison, Jennings Cline, Joe Sullivan, Elizabeth Rich, Martha Myers, Judy Powell, Terry Lydon, Bruce Henderson, and Donna Holman were recognized as National Merit Finalists. Those 11 Lee National Merit Finalists exceeded the number of finalists for all public, independent, private and parochial schools in Montgomery County for the 2013 school year.

After the end of the 1962–63 school year, recognition for earning superior grades was altered so as to recognize students for "Outstanding Scholastic Achievement" and 45 students were pictured in the 1964 *Scabbard*. Glen Seabury, Mike Steeley, Norman Lane, Louisa Martin, Richard Sutliff, Richard Hall, David Meier, and Peter Sanders were recognized as National Merit Finalists.

The 1965 *Scabbard*, the last one of Lee's first decade, recognized Jack Pace, Dick Garrett, Nancy Sowell, Diana Hicks, Jane Moore, Jim Roberts, Bayne Smith, and Tommy McWhorter as National Merit Finalists.

TRADITIONAL VERSUS NONTRADITIONAL EDUCATION

Lemony Snicket writes in *The Blank Book*, "Just because something is traditional is no reason to do it . . ." That is a truism, of course, although some traditional academic practices—such as the offering of classical and modern languages as supplement to the regular curriculum—have evolved into nontraditional practices due to lack of availability.

An outstanding student at Lee High School "back in the day," when classical and modern languages were widely available in public secondary schools and in higher education, is Dr. Peter Howard. An accomplished

Peter Howard

musician and member of the famed John M. Long marching bands at Lee in the '60s, he is a now celebrated professor of such languages at Troy University and a nationally known Latin instructor who consults with academic and military organizations on national testing in the so-called "dead language." In response to a request for a short statement of his memories of his high school's language and related curricula matters and, more generally, what "academics" and its exponents were like in his time at Lee, he submitted the following:

The Lee Academic Atmosphere in the First Decade

By Peter Howard

In forty-five years teaching Latin, Greek and German, I have mentored and read examinations by outstanding students from many of the nation's premiere high schools. I think I know quality when I see it, and I often ask myself what particular factors led to the "high-achieving" school that we ourselves experienced at Robert E. Lee High School during the late 1950s and early 1960s? Students are generally and equally able in any time period and at any location. What then are the keys to outstanding student achievement, and how did the planets line up to bring this about at Lee? Looking back some fifty years through the lens of nostalgia, a few random thoughts as to how and why are:

1. Obviously, some of us were brighter than others, but for the most part we were an "ordinary" student body that studied, worked, and played very hard together to achieve some extraordinary things. There were no "rock stars," and most of us went on to contribute quietly and positively in our respective professions and stations.

2. We benefitted from the extraordinary leadership of T. C. Carlton and Clinton Carter. There was no extreme "fear" factor—we (and the teachers too!) were just expected to behave and to respect their authority. And we were generally well-behaved, aside from an occasional firecracker in the incinerator, a midday visit to Treasure Isle or Dairy Queen, or other

harmless pranks normally associated with youthful exuberance. Even the fabled incident of the garden snake on the lunchroom tray was atypical. In those days, the "board of education" was still liberally applied, and we were well aware of the personalities and techniques of those who wielded it.

3. We benefited immeasurably from a dedicated post-WWII era faculty. We did not really come to know until afterwards how special they were and how many significant things they themselves had accomplished. Recognizing the ability, commitment, and dedication of the teachers, our parents simply entrusted (not abandoned!) us to their care. They supported the school fully, and there was very little "parental interference" in its operation.

4. I don't recall ever hearing a teacher say "If you don't do this, you will fail." We were simply expected to achieve. Likewise, I never heard a teacher or principal use a hackneyed phrase such as "commitment to excellence."

5. An important role was played by students whose parents were stationed at Gunter and Maxwell Air Force Bases. Those students had been out in the world and had gained a broader perspective; they greatly influenced those of us who were "home-grown."

6. Each graduating class must have had a valedictorian and a salutatorian, but I don't recall that ever being a point of special emphasis. National Merit Scholars and Semi-Finalists did receive special recognition in the school annual, but the expectations of the teachers and our own motivation were largely internal.

7. We received and appreciated the support of the public for our endeavors and accomplishments, as demonstrated perennially by the capacity crowds at Cramton Bowl on Friday nights.

8. We benefited from a less-complicated and well-controlled curriculum, and we were genuinely challenged by our teachers. I still remember our Latin teacher Eunice Day often asking, "Will you meet the challenge?"

9. We were often reminded of our predecessors' achievements, and we were expected to maintain that same level of achievement and a proud school tradition.

10. To have been a student in Gladys Nichols's senior English class was in itself a badge of honor. Although I did not have Miss Nichols for English, many of my friends did and I learned much from her, simply by osmosis.

11. We often cheered "We're Number One!" We were in fact the best in many categories, but we didn't flaunt it. One success served as a catalyst for others, and the bleed-over into the classroom from our many accomplishments in athletics and music cannot be over-estimated.

12. The road to achievement did not start at Robert E. Lee. Much credit must be given to our feeder schools Capitol Heights, Goodwyn, and Cloverdale, as well as to the fostering role played by our churches and the community YMCA.

13. As graduates of Robert E. Lee High School, we arrived at our chosen occupations and colleges well prepared, with a strong work ethic, and with a desire to achieve. I remember one night at a rehearsal of the University of Alabama's "Million Dollar Band," the director, Colonel Carleton K. Butler, came over to me and said, "You know, this is just a rehearsal; you don't have to go wide open all of the time." After playing for three years in Johnny Long's "Pride of Dixie" band at Robert E. Lee, however, we didn't know to do anything differently.

14. In summary, I think that the most important factor leading to the collective success of Robert E. Lee High School during this initial ten-year period was simply the fact that "we cared."

A Closing Thought

The first decade of Robert E. Lee High School was highlighted by student success across the spectrum of curricula and non-curricula activities. From academics to extra-curricular activities, most Lee graduates were prepared for lifelong success in a variety of professional and blue-collar fields. Most would give much credit to family, friends, and teachers, and, perhaps, accept a little credit for self-application. It may not have taken a village to educate a teenager in the late 1950s and early 1960s but it did take a number of factors interacting happily at the right place and the right time. Lee High School was such a place, with teachers who became a source of information and insight, inspiration and imagination-enhancing desire to continue learning throughout a lifetime. As the great 19th-century educator Horace Mann reminded, "A human being is not, in any proper sense, a human being till he is educated"—and the process of becoming such is lifelong.

7

The Quality of the Total Program

As Revealed in Academic and Student Activities of the Time

EDITOR'S NOTE: Students at Robert E. Lee High School, even six decades ago, did not just attend classes Monday through Friday, going directly home afterward. No, they enjoyed their interests and passions, just as contemporary students do, in "extracurricular" or "co-curricular activities" and in elective academic programs such as the marching band and choral groups—not to mention the dozens of other "student activities." This chapter on the band, choral department, and selected other student activities reminds us just how busy we were and how profitably and enjoyably engaged.

The Robert E. Lee High School Band, 1955–65

By Kerry Palmer

When planning for the new Robert E. Lee High School, Montgomery school officials realized the importance of music education and its place in a major high school. Yale Ellis had led the Sidney Lanier Poets' band for nearly two decades and had become a recognized figure throughout Alabama. When school officials began planning for Lee High, Ellis was consulted regarding a band program that would befit the fine tradition already present in Montgomery. Cloverdale, Baldwin, and Capitol Heights junior high schools had outstanding bands conducted by fine directors. However, these men did not hold teaching degrees and were

The first Lee band plays at an early Lee Day pep rally in front of the school.

paid based upon band fees charged to the students. When hiring leaders for the high school bands, Montgomery was looking for established directors who had been educated at one of the state's teachers' colleges and preferably a larger institution for graduate school. Montgomery's newest high school was to find such a director through the efforts of Ellis.

During the 1950s, Ellis became closely acquainted with the University of Alabama music department. He worked with Colonel Carlton K. Butler, the director of the famed "Million Dollar Band" and a beloved figure among the state's young band directors. During the summer, Ellis would travel to Tuscaloosa to teach graduate music education courses to high school directors from all over the state as well as instruct high school students at the University's well-known summer music camp. It was in this setting that Ellis met Johnny Long.

A Director Is Named

John Maloy Long was born in Guntersville, Alabama, in 1925. His mother was a fine musician, with a conservatory education. She saw to it that little Johnny began piano lessons at age six. By the seventh grade, he had joined the Marshall County High School band, playing trumpet. By the ninth grade, he was serving as section leader.

In 1943, Long's high school band director was drafted into the Army. The high school principal, fully aware of Johnny's impressive musical abilities, asked him to fill in for the remainder of the year. Johnny did so, and a spectacular teaching career was born.

Upon graduation from high school in 1944, Long was himself drafted into the United States Army. He was assigned to the special services unit to play trumpet in the Southernaires dance band. In addition, Long played the sousaphone in the marching band, as well as other instruments as required by his superiors. Future Lee High School bands would reflect the immense influence of these years of military service. From the name of the school dance band to the look of the marching band uniforms and the ever-present pre-game inspections, a distinct military influence was obvious.

After discharge in 1946, Long enrolled at the University of Alabama in the pre-law program. However, he quickly found that this course of study was not to his liking, as music needed to be more than just a hobby in his life. Consequently, he transferred to Jacksonville State Teachers College, taking the position of band director at Jacksonville Laboratory High School, which paid him $30 per month to lead its program. While at Jacksonville State, Long also assisted with the marching band, directed the ladies' chorus, and formed the Johnny Long Dance

Long as a student at Jacksonville State Teachers College in the 1940s.

Band, playing gigs in Jacksonville, Anniston, and other locales. He graduated with a double major in music and history in 1949.

After graduation, Long became the first full-time band director at Blount County High School in Oneonta, Alabama. It was during his one year there that he met Mary Lynn Adams. Long requested permission from Mr. Adams and the school's principal to date Mary Lynn during the school year. Permission was granted, and the two were married in the summer of 1950.

When Yale Ellis thought of Johnny Long as a candidate for the new Lee High School, Long was entering his fifth year at DeKalb County High School in Fort Payne. The Fort Payne band had earned a statewide reputation under Long's leadership, excelling on the concert stage and innovating on the marching field. Area schools were noticing as were the professors at the University of Alabama, where Long was enrolled as a graduate student. Ellis encouraged Long to apply for the job at the new Montgomery school.

Dr. Clarence Dannelly, superintendent of the school system in Montgomery, sent Ellis to Fort Payne to observe Long's teaching for two days during the fall of 1954. After Ellis returned to Montgomery, Long called Dr. Dannelly and told him that the Fort Payne band had been selected to march in the inaugural parade for Governor Jim Folsom Sr. in January. Dannelly agreed to form a committee to "audition" the band at that parade.

On Robert E. Lee's birthday, January 19, 1955, Dr. Dannelly officially offered the position of Director of Bands at Robert E. Lee High School to John M. Long. This decision would set into motion one of the most impressive ten years of high school band history in the nation.

Long and his young family soon moved to Montgomery and set up housekeeping in an apartment on Spruce Street.

A New Band Is Born

Several members of the east Montgomery community, including Dr. Charles Goodwin and Gus Dozier, assisted with start-up funding for the band. Long quickly arranged for the purchase of marching band uniforms, as well as instruments and music. When money was not available for cases for the school's new sousaphones, Long enlisted shop teacher Guy Medley to build wooden cases. Those cases would remain in use for many years.

Long on the ladder admonishes band members to keep their lines straight during an after-school practice in the fall of 1956.

Some instruments were purchased from Army surplus. A rare 1930s Conn double-belled euphonium was one such example. This instrument was acquired for the hefty sum of $1.

The Lee band was outfitted in beautiful military style uniforms. The band dressed in red double-breasted coats with white pants, white shoes, a black necktie, and a citation cord. Military service caps with plumes topped off the snappy ensemble. Majorettes and flag bearers were outfitted in custom uniforms designed and made by Mrs. Long.

For the first eight years of the band's existence, the group rehearsed beneath the gym in what Long called "the dungeon." The room was cramped and hot, and support columns obstructed the view. This area included an office for the director as well as an equipment storage room, and it had easy access to the practice field adjacent to the school. In early 1964, the band moved into the new auditorium complex, with a large, air-conditioned auditorium space and practice areas for the band and choral departments. The new facility was one of the finest in the state at the time and consisted of 14 rooms, including offices, a music library, a copy room, uniform and instrument storage rooms, several practice rooms, a recording booth, and a

Above: In 1964, the school gained a new auditorium, complete with new areas for the band and choral departments. The 14-room facility was considered the finest then in the state.

spacious band rehearsal room. The facility provided easy access to both the stage and the marching band rehearsal field and is still in use.

THE PRIDE OF DIXIE

Perhaps the best-known component of the Lee music program was the famous Pride of Dixie marching band. This ensemble became known as one of the best of its kind in the nation and was hailed for its innovation and quality of marching and playing. From the beginning, Long wanted the Pride of Dixie to be different, so he went against the grain in an effort to put Lee High School on the map.

Military bands heavily influenced high school and college marching bands during this era. In fact, many college ensembles were ROTC units until after World War II, as was the band at Lanier. In keeping with the military tradition, bands would enter the field at a slow, steady drum cadence, before marching downfield at a pace of 126 beats per minute.

The Lee band's first innovation was the "bombshell entrance." The band members would run onto the field, screaming at the top of their lungs. The announcer would claim that the band was "making its entrance at more than 300 steps per minute," and the crowd would cheer with anticipation.

During his days at Jacksonville State, Long had composed various fanfares.

At Lee, he modified a fanfare originally written for the Jacksonville State band and used it as the opening for most Lee halftime shows during his tenure. The familiar strains of "Dixie" filled Cramton Bowl, and an exciting tradition was born.

The Pride of Dixie executed a precision drill, usually at a quick tempo, to a march. This began every show and was repeated each week throughout the football season. The remainder of the show changed from week to week. Popular music would be centered around a theme. In later years, elaborate props were used, especially when playing Lanier. Long crafted original arrangements especially for the Lee band, using jazz chords to give the band its characteristic sound. The band memorized all halftime show music—another innovation for that era that is practiced almost universally today.

Long made good use of the steep incline of the west stands at Cramton Bowl by designing pictures for the band to form on the field. Musical

The band in formation to open a halftime show with the "Robert E. Lee Fanfare."

arrangements were completed over the weekend, and Long would take his wife and two young children to the school with him on Sunday evenings to run the specific parts on the old mimeograph machine adjacent to the principal's office. The parts would then be ready for the band to rehearse Monday morning. By Thursday, all music and marching for the new show was memorized, and the process would begin anew the following week.

In addition to on-campus rehearsals, the Lee band made use of Yancey Park. Many summer rehearsals were held in the early morning to avoid the

Below: The 1956 Pride of Dixie Marching Band.

heat of the day. Sometimes, the band would rehearse well into the evening. As daylight faded, Long would have students pull cars up to the front of the field and turn on their headlights so the band could keep going. As the years passed, people would gather to watch the band in rehearsal. Many future Lee band members were introduced to the band in this way.

The Lee band began to travel as soon as school opened in 1955. During the band's inaugural season, Long arranged to have the band perform for halftime at the Jacksonville State Teachers College homecoming game. Long had been somewhat of a celebrity at his alma mater, and he and his new band were welcomed back with open arms. The first edition of the *Stars*

and Bars features a picture of the Pride of Dixie on the front page, complete with a full report of the trip. During the remaining years of Long's tenure, the Lee band was invited to perform at halftime at Auburn University, Troy State College, and Jacksonville State College. The band also provided halftime entertainment for the Alabama All-Star Football Game held at the University of Alabama.

LEE-LANIER SHOWS

When Lee began playing Lanier, halftime shows became more and more extravagant, with the Lee band unveiling large props, designed and built by mechanical drawing teacher Hagan King, for each performance. By the 1960s, Cramton Bowl was packed to capacity, with tickets sold out in August of each year. Fans remained in the stands for halftime, and neither band disappointed.

The 1960 Lee band performed "An Arabian Knight's Fantasy" for the Lanier game. The band formed Aladdin's lamp, a mosque, Egyptian pyramids,

A show based on the music and traditions of Hawaii during a Lee vs. Lanier halftime in the early 1960s.

The Generals honor their crosstown rivals, the Lanier Poets.

and the sword of an Arabian knight on the field, filling the air with selections such as "In a Persian Market," "Caravan," "Valley of the Kings," and "The Sheikh of Arabie." In 1961, the band presented a Hawaiian show, complete with a functioning volcano belching billows of smoke throughout the show. In 1962, the band went with a Dixieland theme, forming a cotton bale and moving musical notes as the band played and danced to the "Dixieland One-Step." This particular show featured an oversized functioning riverboat, complete with a working paddle wheel. The riverboat was appropriately named the "Goodship Robert E. Lee."

In 1963, a large train with a working smokestack entered the stadium as the band presented a railroad show. The band formed two colliding trains on the field and presented "The Legend of Casey Jones," along with the familiar strains of "I've Been Working on the Railroad," "Night Train," and "Alabammy Bound."

The Long era ended in October 1964 with a salute to Southern states. A replica of the Alabama Capitol was rolled onto the field as the "Pride of Dixie" saluted their special guest, Governor George C. Wallace, with "Stars Fell on Alabama." These exciting shows were a significant part of the Lee-Lanier rivalry and are remembered fondly today.

Three Summer 1958 Highlights: Top, performing at the Lions International Convention in Chicago. Middle, as the Alabama official representative, leading the Lions International Parade. Inset, Long accepts the "First Chair in America" award from Superintendent Walter McKee.

The Blue-Gray Game

In October 1955, Long was approached by Champ Pickens, executive director of the Blue-Gray Football Classic sponsored by the Montgomery Lions Club. Long was offered $50 to organize pregame and halftime festivities for this long-standing nationally televised football game. He immediately accepted and would serve in this capacity for nearly fifty years, with his pay increasing incrementally over time.

Long immediately contacted his good friend Bobby Collins, who had replaced Yale Ellis at Lanier. The two agreed to share performing duties each December. Over time, the halftime festivities expanded greatly. The University of Southern Mississippi Pride of Mississippi Marching Band was a frequent performer, and a "massed band" of thousands of high school students from all over the state eventually became a feature of the game. The Lee and Lanier bands would often combine on the field, especially during pregame shows. They played the "Alabama State Song," the "Star Spangled Banner," and "Dixie" together on these occasions. The Lee band continued as a regular performer for the Blue-Gray game through the 1990s, making it the most televised high school band in the nation during that time period.

National Contests

During Long's ten-year span at Lee, the band participated in five national contests throughout the United States and Canada. Remarkably, they never placed lower than fourth in these competitions, and they won the top prize at the 1961 VFW National Parade Competition in Miami Beach.

In 1958, the band made its first venture onto the national stage by entering the Lions International Parade Competition in Chicago. This contest was held in conjunction with the Lions Club International Convention. Some 126 bands from 96 nations entered the contest, with the Lee band finishing in fourth place.

The band raised money for this trip by selling "World's Finest Chocolate" bars and soliciting donations. For the parade, the band wore Confederate soldier uniforms consisting of gray coveralls and a yellow sash (sewn for each member by Mrs. Long). Confederate souvenir caps were purchased, complete with crossed pistols on the front. The band also wore their "Pride of

A 1964 edition of the Lee newspaper celebrates one of the band's national contest victories.

Dixie" shoulder patches and citation cords, along with white military boots.

Long arranged a rousing rendition of "Dixie" especially for this trip. The now-iconic arrangement began with a bold, low brass statement of the opening bars of "Dixie," transitioning to a brief trumpet fanfare from "The Battle Hymn of the Republic." The band then launched into an aggressive up-tempo rendition of "Dixie," with the strains of "Sewanee River" played by the low brass as a partner song underneath the melody. The arrangement concluded with the low brass restating the "Dixie" melody with gusto, accompanied by the percussion section. This new musical selection became an instant hit with fans, and was taken to Troy State by Long in 1965 where it served for years as that school's fight song.

For national parade competitions, the Lee band executed a precision street drill, complete with flashy marching maneuvers and dance steps. In 1961, upon the advice of Dr. Paul Yoder, the Lee band performed "The Chicago Tribune" as the parade selection. While not normally played on

The Quality of the Total Program

the march, Dr. Yoder, a world-renowned composer and band director, suggested that this particular selection would be a showstopper due to its intricate woodwind parts and smooth, soft brass feature in the middle. Yoder felt that this complex concert march would let the Lee band showcase its tremendous versatility, thus giving the band an advantage over the loud, brassy drum and bugle corps which would be Lee's primary competition.

To maximize the musical effect, Long and Lee drum major George Hammett walked the parade route the day before the competition, carefully determining where the band would need to begin playing the march to time the musical climax with the band's arrival at the reviewing stand. During the parade, the timing worked perfectly, with the band dropping to a whisper upon its approach to the judges' seating area. All woodwinds and percussion members stopped playing, and the brass section played the lush strains of the trio as softly as possible. Then, without warning—and right on time—the whole ensemble came in at full volume to finish the piece in dramatic fashion. The result was a first-place finish and the declaration that the Robert E. Lee Band was the "number one band in the nation." Supporters organized a parade through downtown Montgomery to welcome the victorious band home; Long was presented a new car for this noble achievement.

Other national appearances during this era included trips to Detroit, Cleveland, and New Orleans for national contests. The 1964 Cleveland trip was an epic journey, with significant side trips. In New York, the band performed at the World's Fair. Then it was on to Washington where the band presented a concert on the steps of the U.S. Capitol. It was said that audience members "threw their hats in the air" as the band completed the program with their by then famous rendition of "Dixie."

The Concert Band

While more people saw and heard the Pride of Dixie, the Robert E. Lee Concert Band was truly remarkable and made a significant impact at both the state and national levels. Playing only literature of the highest quality, membership in the concert band required students to be true musicians.

Members of the Lee band were exposed to the great concert band composers and arrangers of the day, as well as legendary orchestral composers, through the many transcriptions programmed by the band. The band entered the district band festival each year of Long's tenure and participated in the State Band Contest at the University of Alabama for nine years. The Robert E. Lee Band was the only band in Alabama to receive Superior ratings in class AA for six consecutive years during this period. People would fill Foster Auditorium at the University of Alabama to hear the Lee band's performance, which was usually near the end of the final day of the contest. During this time, the Lee band was considered by many to be the finest in the state. In addition to performing locally, the concert band played at most of the band's national contest appearances throughout this 10-year span and also presented a concert at the Instrumental Conductor's Conference at the University of Southern Mississippi in 1964.

During Long's tenure at Lee, the band set the state record for the number of All-State first- and second-chair medals earned in a given year. In 1958, 23 members of the concert band sat first or second chair in the All-State band. No band before or since has achieved this distinction. Lee led the state in All-State first- and second-chair medals for most of the first 10 years of the school's existence.

The early success of the Lee marching and concert bands, coupled with its impressive All-State representation, caught the attention of the John Phillip Sousa Foundation. This group, dedicated to promoting and rewarding the highest quality in band programs nationwide, added the Lee band to its Historic Honor Roll of Bands from 1920–60. The Lee band is the only band from Alabama so listed for this time period. In later years, Long served on the board of directors for this prestigious organization and would be awarded the foundation's highest award, the Sudler Medal of Honor, after his retirement.

Southernaires and Lancers

When organizing the Lee band in 1955, Long felt that the study of jazz was an important component of a well-rounded musical education. Most school band programs during this era focused exclusively on marching and concert programs. However, Long's emphasis on jazz created enough interest

Top, the Southernaires. Bottom, the Lancers.

among students to fully assemble two dance bands.

The Southernaires and Lancers were organized by Long, but much responsibility was given to students for the management and direction of these ensembles. Over time, these groups were in high demand at school dances and community events. The Southernaires once played at Redstone Arsenal in Huntsville and had the opportunity to meet Wernher von Braun, the famous rocket scientist. Members of the Southernaires went on to play in the two most accomplished university dance bands in the state during this period, the Alabama Cavaliers and the Auburn Knights. At one time, the

Working for perfection, the band does it "one more time" after school during the 1950s.

entire trumpet section in the Cavaliers consisted of former Southernaires.

LIFE LESSONS

Former members of Long's bands at Lee will tell you that he taught as much about life as he did about music. He was known as the consummate motivator and was credited with pushing his students to achieve above and beyond their wildest expectations. A look at the accomplishments of former band members during the Long era reveals a plethora of career fields and a tremendous level of success. Lee band alumni have excelled in musical and nonmusical careers. Former members hold faculty positions in distinguished music schools around the country and are professional musicians, doctors, surgeons, lawyers, engineers, accountants, and dentists. They all speak of Long's folksy manner of giving advice—lovingly referred to today as "Longisms." Some of the most memorable are:

"Always remember to use those three magic words: 'Please, thank you, and yes, sir or no, sir.'"

"You are just as good as Winston Churchill—not any better."

"Better never than late!"

"Things have not changed in a thousand years."

"If you think you're indispensable, go down to the graveyard and I'll show you lots of other people who thought they were, too."

"Find the hardest thing you can do, then do it. You will be successful."

"If you think you're special, stick your hand in a bucket of water. If you pull it out and leave a hole, you're special."

"You'll have to play louder! There's somebody sitting on the bank eating popcorn."

"Plugs want soft soap; champions, criticism." (This saying adorned a sign that hung in the band room during the Long years.)

Long's Farewell

In December 1964, Dr. Charles Farmer, head of the music department at Troy State College, approached Long as the band sat in the stands during the annual Blue Gray game at Cramton Bowl. Ralph W. Adams had begun his tenure as president at Troy State in October and had quickly surmised that the school was in desperate need of a new band director. Upon the advice of mutual friend Governor George Wallace, Adams had been in contact with Long in the previous weeks regarding a move to Troy. Long had repeatedly reminded Adams that he was happy at Lee and did not want to move. A job offer from Troy was nothing new for Long as the college had approached him during the late '50s and had finally given up after several refusals.

Caught off guard by Dr. Farmer, and fully aware of the status of the band at Troy, Long again refused the offer. However, Dr. Farmer had strict orders to find out what it would take to get the Lee director to part with the program he loved so much. After a brief conversation, the two men began looking for something on which to write out Long's "demands." A discarded peanut sack was found, and Long proceeded to request things that he was sure no small, liberal arts college in south Alabama could ever fulfill: full professorship, new instruments, new uniforms, a large travel budget, and a massive increase in salary. Long handed the bag back to Dr. Farmer who looked it over carefully for a couple of moments, lifted his head and said, "Anything else?"

By January 1965, Long's signature was on a contract and he was on his way to making history at Troy. Over the next few years, many members of the Lee band followed Long to Troy, helping him to grow the Sound of the South from a membership of 75 when he arrived to more than 200 in the fall of 1970.

In 1971, Long was offered the job as band director at the University of Alabama but decided to remain at Troy when he was offered the position of Dean of the College of Arts and Sciences. That same year, he was presented with an honorary doctorate by his alma mater, Jacksonville State University. By the time he retired in 1997, the band boasted over 300 members, and the band building was named in his honor. The music school at Troy is now known as the John M. Long School of Music, and a street in Troy bears his name. In 1977, he was elected to membership in the Alabama Bandmasters Hall of Fame, and in 1995 he was inducted into the National Band Association Hall of Fame of Distinguished Band Conductors. Long was inducted into the first class of the Robert E. Lee Hall of Fame in 1994.

Johnny Long's ten years at Lee High School will forever be hailed as a decade of excellence among high school bands. In no time at all, the band achieved national recognition and propelled its director into what has become one of the most coveted band jobs in the nation at Troy University. The Lee band's impressive contest record for 1955–65 is listed below. It serves as a tangible representation of the quality of the band program.

Robert E. Lee High School Band Contest Record
1955–56
- Organized by John M. Long and nicknamed the Pride of Dixie
- Band did not enter the State Contest the first year
- 9 first- and second-chair medals – All-State – University of Alabama

1957
- Superior – State Contest – University of Alabama
- 14 first- and second-chair medals – All-State – University of Alabama
- Presented halftime show at Alabama Polytechnic Institute (now Auburn University)

1958
- Superior – State Contest – University of Alabama
- 23 first- and second-chair medals – All-State – University of Alabama
- Led entire state
- All-time record held by all bands in Alabama
- Fourth in the nation – Lion's International Parade – Chicago
- Presented halftime show at the All Star Football Game – University of Alabama

1959
- Superior – State Contest – University of Alabama
- 21 first- and second-chair medals – All-State – University of Alabama
- Led the entire state
- Presented halftime show at the All Star Football Game – University of Alabama

1960
- Superior – State Contest – University of Alabama
- 20 first- and second-chair medals – All-State – University of Alabama
- Led the entire state
- Third in the Nation – VFW National Contest – Detroit
- Presented a concert in Windsor, Canada
- Listed in the John Philip Sousa Foundation's "Historic Honor Roll of Bands" from 1920–60; only Alabama band so honored during this period

1961
- Superior – State Contest – University of Alabama
- 20 first- and second-chair medals – All-State – University of Alabama
- Led entire state
- First in the Nation – VFW Military Parade Contest – Miami

1962
- Superior – State Contest – University of Alabama
- 19 first- and second-chair medals – All-State – University of Alabama
- Led entire state

1963
- Excellent – State Contest – University of Alabama
- 11 first- and second-chair medals – All-State – University of Alabama

1964
- Superior – State Contest – University of Alabama
- 11 first- and second-chair medals – All-State – University of Alabama
- Presented a concert at the Instrumental Conductor's Conference – University of Southern Mississippi
- Official band for the State of Alabama – World's Fair – New York
- Presented a concert on the steps of the U.S. Capitol – Washington
- Second in the nation – VFW National Contest – Cleveland

1965
- Superior – State Contest – University of Alabama
- 9 first- and second-chair medals – All-State – University of Alabama
- First Runner-Up – "Greatest Bands in Dixie" Parade – New Orleans, LA

1955–62
- Official band of the Blue-Gray All Star Football Classic broadcast nationally by NBC

1958–65
- "First Chair of America" National Yearbook for high school bands

WITH HIS DEPARTURE, LONG recommended 1960 Lee graduate Thomas R. Borden to assume the directorship of the band. Borden guided the Lee band with excellence for the next 15 years, including the trying time of integration that soon follow Long's exit. Under Borden, the Robert E. Lee High School Band continued to perform with the high level of excellence established at its founding.

The Band Takes a Northern Tour

By Clinton Carter

In the summer of 1964, I was in my second year as the vice principal of Robert E. Lee High School. By 1964 the Lee band had made quite a name for itself. The band, under the direction of the legendary John M. Long, had been invited to compete in a three-day competition in Cleveland, Ohio, sponsored by the Veterans of Foreign Wars. More than 100 bands and drill teams were to compete.

I was assigned by Principal Tim Carlton to serve as one of the chaperones. Another assignment was to carry a large amount of cash ($10,000 as I recall) to feed the band members and to pay for incidental expenses. I had all this in a bank bag that I carried the entire trip, sticking it inside my coat when outside the bus and stashing it under the mattress in the hotels (Try that today!).

We departed Montgomery in early morning for this 11-day trip, boarding three aging buses and heading north. Band members were dressed in

Members of the Pride of Dixie, dressed in Confederate uniforms, board the bus on their epic 1964 championship tour

Gladys Nichols, Johnny Long, and Clinton Carter pose in front of a Trailways bus during the 1964 summer band tour.

Confederate-gray uniforms with caps much like those worn during the Civil War.

There was no means of communication between the buses and they were not restroom-equipped. Everyone then fell under the mercy of Johnny Long in the lead bus as he was the one to decide when and where to make rest stops. As I recall, he dozed off as soon as his bus started and only came to life when his camel bladder dictated a stop.

I don't think the elderly driver of my bus had been north of Elmore County. His driving could best be described as erratic if not downright dangerous. Remember that this was in the years before anything like a complete interstate road system was in place. As we crossed into Tennessee, we encountered rain and in one of the small towns my bus skidded off the street and came to a stop with its door about a foot from the front porch of a house. I recall a lady coming out of her door and onto the porch. The driver opened the door, and without the need to get out of his seat, expressed his apology for damaging her lawn. Most of the luggage in the overhead bins had been dumped on us and it took some time to get things back in order and return to the road.

We made a brief stop in Cleveland, Tennessee, where the band took time to stretch and to do a short rehearsal, including the playing of "Dixie." Much to my relief we also changed drivers.

Continuing north, we made no more stops, with the exception of restroom and snack breaks, until we arrived in Cleveland, Ohio, and checked into our hotel. We took in a professional baseball game. From the performance of the pitchers it didn't seem that anyone was on steroids. The band won second-place in the competition, receiving a nice trophy and $800 in cash, but no one topped them in the playing of "Dixie" or in the waving of the Stars and Bars flag.

Leaving Cleveland late in the day we drove directly to New York City, again with only infrequent stops for restrooms and snacks. Our driver was fairly young and I thought I could finally relax and sleep. Much to my dismay we found that he could barely stay awake at the wheel. We rotated several band members to stand at his side to keep him talking and were finally forced to have an on-board nurse break ammonia capsules under his nose.

We had a great time in New York, the seedy hotel notwithstanding. The band toured the Statue of Liberty, the Empire State Building, Chinatown, and the Worlds Fair, where the band performed. Most of the audience seemed to have enjoyed "Dixie." Two of our bus drivers wanted to ride the subway and we were delayed while they tried to figure out how to get back to their starting point.

From New York we made our way to Washington, D.C. We visited Arlington National Cemetery, the Custis-Lee Mansion, the grave of President Kennedy, the Lincoln Memorial, and the Washington Monument. All this was capped off with a concert on the steps of the Capitol where the band played "Dixie" and waved the Stars and Bars.

We then headed south to Montgomery. We made a stop in Richmond, Virginia to refuel the buses. The bus I was riding had a bad clutch and we failed to make it to the top of the inclined off-ramp. It was only after all the boys got off to lighten the load that we limped to the top.

From Richmond we continued our trip down through the Smoky Mountains, arriving at the steps of the Capitol in Montgomery to the cheers of parents and hundreds of supporters. The band played "Dixie" and waved

The Lee band was treated to a welcome home rally on the steps of the State Capitol upon their triumphant return in 1964.

the Stars and Bars.

We experienced very few discipline problems with band members during the entire trip. We just turned them loose. I do recall having been awakened one night with a report that a couple of boys were in a room housing four girls. Upon investigation the students told me that they were only discussing who would teach their algebra class. I believed them, since Lee students were at that time too morally grounded to tell a lie.

Within a few days after the end of the trip, the 1964–65 school year started. There was an assembly of students and faculty in the newly constructed auditorium, the first use of that facility. Mr. Carlton and I, along with other faculty members, tried to ease the anxieties related to the fact that within a day or two we were to enroll four African American students, another first—and perhaps the most far-reaching—in the history of the school.

The new Confederate-type uniforms went into mothballs and were eventually given away over the years. "Dixie" gradually faded away as did the waving of the Stars and Bars. Johnny Long left Lee for Troy University and I have stuck to my commitment not to ride a bus more than 30 miles for the remainder of my life.

My career with Montgomery Public Schools spanned 49 years. With no hesitation I can say that the first two years I spent at Lee (1962–63 and 1963–64) were the most rewarding, including that long bus ride. I can only describe the atmosphere at Lee during those years as having been electric. The energy among the student body, the faculty, the parents, and the hundreds of community supporters was something that I have never experienced again.

Thoughts on Ellyn G. Dudley and the Choral Department

By Tom Hammett

A common sentiment among alums of the period is that the early days of Robert E. Lee High School were "The Days of Camelot." That is especially so among the musically inclined, such as my Hammett family.

The Hammetts moved in 1954 to Bradley Drive, just about three blocks from the site of the soon-to-be-built high school on Ann Street. I remember playing around the construction site, filling my pockets with the coin-looking slugs from electrical boxes, and marveling at the rebar, lumber, concrete blocks, plywood and nearly endless construction materials. It was a kid's paradise!

In the fall of 1955, Johnny Long began working with a group of neighborhood kids who would grow into a national championship band that would be the center of the lives of hundreds of students for many years to come. The spirited sound of the band could be heard each afternoon throughout the neighborhood, and it lured a good number of fans to the practice field sidelines each afternoon. I was immediately hooked and spent the next twelve years of my life in and around the band that was my primary social, musical, and academic outlet.

Following in the steps of the already famous Hammett Brothers, I was tagged by students and faculty as "Little Hammett." I became somewhat of a band mascot. I was especially attracted to the drumline; guys like John Harrison, Jim Dinkins, George McCain, and Johnny Haynes became my musical heroes. By the fifth grade, Dr. Long allowed me a spare uniform to wear in the stands and when I traveled with the band to away games. Jim Dinkins would often let me play on his drum so he could better watch the game. Man, what a thrill!

When I arrived as a sophomore student in fall of 1964, we were called to the new auditorium for a class orientation meeting. Principal Tim Carlton spoke, along with the other officials. Near the end of the meeting Mr. Carlton looked out where I was sitting with some buddies on the 10th row and said, "Oh, I see my friend Little Hammett sitting out there. How long have you been playing the drums, Little Hammett?" I mumbled shyly, "About 10 years." He asked me to repeat what I had said. I spoke up loudly and said, "Oh, I don't know!" He said in front of the group he wanted to see me in his office after the assembly. When I met with him he was friendly but firm. What I remembered from the conversation was his statement, "If you ever make an 'F' at Robert E. Lee, I'm going to wear your butt out!" I was a believer!

As school progressed, I was on track toward becoming a band director as brothers Willie and George had done. Ken had taken an academic engineering path. A seed had been planted in my musical ear a year or two earlier by the Lee High Choral Department. Prior to the construction of the Lee auditorium and music facilities, the Glee Club and Choralees held their concerts in the auditorium of Capitol Heights Junior High school, where I was then a student. I enjoyed the concerts very much. Something about those wonderfully blended voices in selections of a wide variety of music, and the happy atmosphere, caught my ear and heart like nothing else. Soloists such as Suzie Stephens and groups like Generals Three added such sweet icing to the choral cake.

My first involvement with the choruses happened as I was asked to accompany some soloists and groups in a combo on my drums. It didn't take long for my interest and involvement to expand exponentially. I joined the two major ensembles, Choralees and Glee Club and expanded my network of musical friends by dozens and dozens! We had a stable of highly accomplished accompanists: Rob Parker, Carol Palmer, Betty Burkett, and six or eight more pianists

Ellyn Dudley served as choral director at Lee High School from 1955 until her death in 1974.

The 1964–65 Choralees.

provided an amazing foundation of accompaniment. Singers such as Ann Small, Betty Spruell Sandra Denham, Frieda Crumpler, Eddie Wohlford, and David Hoit helped create a musical ensemble.

Similar to the cult-like following of Johnny Long, Ellyn Dudley was the heart and catalyst around which the Choral Department revolved. I guess we had over 200 students involved in the various groups, with the Choralees being the select ensemble. Miss Dudley's most outstanding quality was that she loved each and every student and provided an atmosphere wherein each student could thrive and succeed. She was a highly qualified and experienced choral director. She provided an exhaustive repertory of choral literature that ranged from the latest popular songs, folk songs, and spirituals to the highest quality choral classics. She made opportunities for individuals to sing solos in all styles. Groups like Girls' Trio, Boys' Quartet, Barbershoppers, and Lettermen-like trios were highly encouraged and given opportunities for public performance.

The attraction of the Glee Club and Choralees was quite extraordinary. Students were required to have a study hall in their schedules in those days, and a number of students sang with the choir during fifth-period study hall. I secured a "permanent pass" from study hall to attend chorus classes. So, for my years of choral involvement, I never received any academic credit or grades. What I did receive was vastly more valuable than a couple of credits.

The Glee Club singing for students at a Thanksgiving assembly in 1958.

Before-school rehearsals were the norm. That was when the Choralees rehearsed as a non-credit ensemble. Pop groups such as the Generals Three and Girl Watchers trios rehearsed after school as time would permit.

I believe it was my junior year that Miss Dudley asked me to go to the front of the room and conduct a selection. Oh, no, it couldn't be something simple like a folk song or spiritual. It was Haydn's "The Heavens Are Telling" from *Creation*! I had no trouble conducting the 4/4 time and bluffing my way through the first couple of pages, but when I looked up from the score and saw 80 singers looking right at me, it scared me to death. I didn't look up again for the remainder of the song. I'm not sure I'm fully recovered to this day.

It was a different time in the 1950s and '60s. One Saturday afternoon I parked close to the music building where I noticed an open window. I stood on the car and pulled myself up through the open window and spent the next several hours reorganizing and alphabetizing the entire choral library. Come Monday morning, I was called to the office concerning breaking into the school over the weekend. Mr. Carlton didn't know quite what to do with me, but I do remember the situation blew over with little or no consequence. This was an example of the loyalty that Ellyn Dudley engendered.

Like all aspects of life at Lee High, standards of music excellence were expected in every undertaking in the Choral Department. We just assumed

Rehearsal in the original choral music classroom.

we would master every note of every song, sing with musical artistry, and thrill every audience. I remember the auditorium was filled to capacity at every concert. One or two years we participated in the Singing Christmas Tree at Garrett Coliseum, a memorable experience with that 60-foot "tree" that held scores of singers. I'll never forget the young lady occupying the top angel spot who fainted near the end of the concert. Eddie and I scaled the emptying structure and helped her to floor level. Miss Dudley led this citywide Christmas music extravaganza with grace, elegance and excitement.

Teachers were required by state education regulations to teach a few life values in addition to their subject content and had to sign a statement to that effect each month prior to receiving their paychecks. Each month Miss Dudley would come to class and say, "Don't smoke, don't drink, and be kind to animals." With that, she could sign her form with a clear conscience.

There are those special teachers in lucky students' lives who are the game changers, who possess almost indescribable qualities of humanity and become the hooks on which every important facet of life hangs. Miss Dudley, with her quiet humility, was one of those life-changers.

Those three years of unparalleled, amazing days at Robert E. Lee went by all too soon. When I arrived at Troy, of course the first two classes for which I registered were Collegiate Singers and Marching Band.

During the summer of 1974 I received a call in Troy that Miss Dudley had been hospitalized with advanced-stage cancer. I made a number of trips to Montgomery to visit her and was admitted to her intensive care room many times, even when family members were not permitted. I was not particularly well-equipped to deal with such a beloved teacher and friend in her terminal condition, but we enjoyed moments of mutual appreciation and love. I was honored to serve as a pallbearer at her funeral.

The doors opened through Ellyn Dudley blazed my trail to the finest choral opportunities in the world. Singing and touring with the Troy Collegiate Singers, doctoral studies, and concerts with outstanding ensembles at Florida State University, many years of concerts with Maestro Robert Shaw, including appearances in Carnegie Hall and Lincoln Center—along with being part of numerous Grammy Award-winning recordings with the Symphony Chorus—all began in the hallowed halls of the Robert E. Lee High School Music Department, band and chorus.

It is the collective thought of many alumni that what we experienced in the early years at Lee High was truly unique—the right place at the right time, with an extraordinary faculty, an extraordinary student body, and unparalleled opportunities to perform. As a number of Alabamians have told me in recent years, Robert E. Lee High School and its students were legends throughout the state. I suppose the academic offerings and opportunities were equally stellar, but I am certain the opportunities offered in the Instrumental and Choral Music Departments were the very best possible. I am thankful to have participated in both.

Student Activities: "May I Have your Attention Please?"

EDITOR'S NOTE: STUDENTS, EVEN Lee band students, do not live by musical notation alone. Sometimes, they are required to practice, eat, sleep, and to engage in all of the other sorts of activities that public school students are heir to. Accordingly, they were given opportunities on a regularly scheduled basis to take part in dozens of clubs and in other non-academic activities, before, during, or after regular curricular activities. In the following pages, the authors well describe the range and nature of those activities at Lee back in the late fifties and early sixties, even putting them into the appropriate cultural, entertainment, and social contexts.

BY ROBIN BOZEMAN HARDWICH AND DEBBIE KNIGHT HOOKS

While academics would be the inherent reason to start a new school, book knowledge alone does not make a person successful, wealthy, and perhaps even wise. There is so much more to an education than simply having facts and knowledge in one's head. Leadership skills, work skills, athletic skills, business skills, life skills,

French Club students participate in the 1959 Lee Day Parade.

and social skills, to name a few, are often learned outside the traditional classroom and found in extracurricular activities and social opportunities. Dee-Dee Givens, Secretary of the Junior Class, said it well in the 1961 Junior Class Message in the *Scabbard* when she wrote, "We face the future with confidence because we know the knowledge we gain at Lee will be a guide in our lives and in our future."

Hence, there follows a need to offer clubs, organizations, work opportunities, athletic events, dances, volunteer service activities, writing opportunities, and creative arts activities. Thus the educational institution developed programs where students could develop lifelong skills which helped them develop into productive adults in their future jobs, their future marriages, their areas of recreational interests, and their interest in community services.

The first *Scabbard* staff (1956) used the theme "The Showboat," and in that first yearbook a section was dedicated to "Activities." Marie Little, Secretary of the first Senior Class of Robert E. Lee, wrote in that first *Scabbard* that they ". . .entered to learn; we leave to serve." Having opportunities to hold offices in clubs, to plan dances and other social events, being involved in professional organizations, or participating in actual work experiences led to teaching students how to be productive adults. Like all high schools, Robert E. Lee would go through years of graduating students that would become famous writers, doctors, lawyers, politicians, educators, coaches, business men and women, wives, husbands, preachers, parents, ministers, and other contributing members of society. Many got their start in various clubs and organizations offered through the school. Many thanks are in order to the faculty and staff that worked diligently to start up all these various and important "activities" that made high school years so memorable.

It seemed every subject in school had a club. There was the Library Club, Latin Club, French Club, Spanish Club, Home Economics Club, Dramatics Club (later known by various other names such as the La Dram in 1961 and Thespian Club in 1963, one of the largest clubs at Lee), to name a few. The 1965 *Scabbard* published the purpose of the Thespian Troupe as "to develop dramatic talent and the art of acting, to cultivate a taste for the best in the drama, and to foster the cultural values, which dramatics develops." In 1957 the Biology Club, the Chemistry Club, Physics Club,

The Senior Girls Tea.

and Future Homemakers of America were added. By October 1962 the *Stars and Bars* mentioned the first meeting held by a new club, the Junior Classical League. Again, opportunities for students to elect officers, attend events and programs, and send delegates to state conventions began. The purpose of this organization for Latin students was to "promote interest in Greek and Roman classics and customs."

For students more interested in working right after graduation, there were clubs that gave one an opportunity to have a job during part of the school day. Two such organizations were the Diversified Occupation and Distributive Education clubs. These were not clubs that were designed for all work and no play. The first D.O. Club sold Christmas cards to pay for various activities, one of which was a Valentine's Party. The March 1962 *Stars and Bars* mentioned that D.O. clubs held district competitions at Auburn University with essay, oratorical, job projects, and job manual contests. At that time, the Lee D.O. Club had been chosen the most outstanding club in the Southeastern district for five consecutive years. Members also participated in various contests where winners attended state conventions at the University of Alabama. The Commercial Club invited local business leaders to speak to their members in preparation for the work world which would follow after graduation.

The YMCA was also a very important part of high school life during 1955–65. Hi-Y (men's clubs) and Tri Hi-Y groups (girls' clubs) provided opportunities for leadership roles, community service venues, and dances and parties. A favorite activity of the Y clubs was a hayride or "function" to Camp Rotary (now named Camp Chandler) on Lake Jordan. Students were quick to discuss the importance of God in their Hi-Y and Tri Hi-Y groups. In 1965, Ron Davenport, Lee student body president, was elected president of the national Hi-Y organization at the annual convention held in Northfield, Minnesota, representing about 350,000 Hi-Y members across the nation. The purpose of this organization, as reported in the September issue of the *Stars and Bars* (1965), was "to create, maintain, and extend throughout the home, school, and community high standards of Christian character." These clubs offered service projects in their communities.

Many more groups were formed during Lee's second year. There was also the beginning of religious clubs in 1957 with the formation of the Inspiration Club. There was even a page in the *Scabbard* donated to pictures of local churches where Lee High students worshiped. By 1963 there were six different devotional clubs, which shows how important church and religion was in our high schools during this time. In the 1961 *Scabbard* the purpose of the Inspiration Club or devotional clubs as they were later referred to in the Lee annuals, was "to create throughout the student body an attitude of Christian spirit."

The Senior Girls' Club was begun the first year Lee opened its doors. The purpose of this club was to show Lee spirit, create an atmosphere of friendliness, and support all school activities. The members sponsored a Girls' tea for all newcomers, entertained the student body with a dance, eventually sponsored the Christmas tree in the lobby, and conducted Twirp Week. During Twirp Week, usually in March, girls raced to the lobby to buy Twirp privileges for 25 cents. Buying this license, girls were allowed to talk to boys, ask them for dates, and carry their books. According to the *Stars and Bars*, if a girl was caught without a license, she was summoned to court and then judged. The week culminated with the Twirp Dance and the revealing of the Twirp King. With funds raised by the club, the Senior

Dances were frequent and popular activities during the first decade at Lee High School. Top, students enjoy the 1955 Halloween dance. Above, an unidentified dance. Next page, top, the 1963 Twirp Dance, and bottom, the 1963 Junior-Senior Prom.

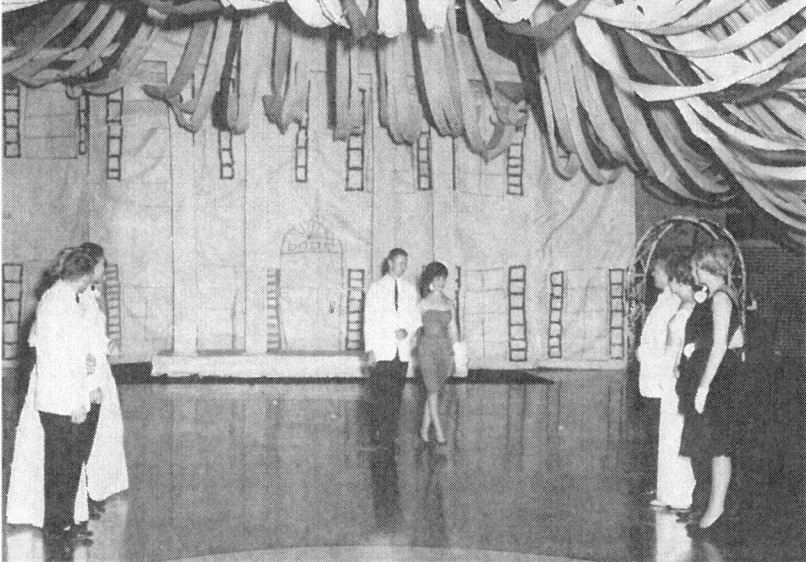

Girls' Club of 1956 donated two sterling ladles that were among the first heirlooms of Robert E. Lee High School.

By 1958, the Future Teachers of America was added to clubs and activities at Lee. Their goal was to promote interest in teaching as a vocation. Other clubs added this year included the Junior/Senior Inspiration Club, new Hi-Y and Tri Hi-Y clubs, Choralees, and the Music Appreciation Club. The Glee Club was intended for all who wanted to sing individually and in a group. There were other music groups, too, such as Girls' Ensemble and Four Part Women's Music. The Robert E. Lee Band was led by the famous

Johnny Long and the dance band during this time was the Southernaires. A dance orchestra known as the Lancers began in 1961.

Other clubs and organizations begun in the first 10 years of Robert E. Lee history include the Radio Club, Scribblettes, Art Club, Barbell Club, Twirlers, Flag Bearers, Advertising Staff, Lee Leaders Club (sponsored through the East Montgomery YMCA), Girl Scout Troop 33 (1963), Numismatists Club (1965), and Program Service Club (1965), to name a few more. The

Top, the first edition of the Pride of Dixie marches in the inaugural Lee Day Parade. Bottom, a Lee Day float in the fall of 1957.

Miss Lee High and her court, 1964.

International Relations Club began in 1961 to create interest and understanding in world affairs. To quote the leadership of this club in the 1961 *Scabbard*, "the significant challenge to 'Young America' is that their role of leadership can be defined only after a careful analysis and study of the way of life of neighboring nations. Today all nations are neighbors of necessity." One of their first projects was to raise funds to support CARE. All of these various clubs and organizations had a central purpose, to build leadership skills and to help students become well rounded and good citizens in their communities wherever life took them.

Parties and Dances

Where there was a club there was usually a party or dance sometime during the year. Socializing was a favorite part of activities at Lee. Dances and parties in 1955–56 were held almost every month. The first dance was held the night before the first all-day session at Robert E. Lee. A rope of colored lights skirted the parking area in front of the school. As old and new friends chatted, a Rock-ola played lively music. Coaches, football players, majorettes, and cheerleaders were all introduced.

Other dances included Halloween, post-game football dances, Lee

Day, Mardi Gras, Beauty Ball (at Christmas), Twirp, the most anticipated Junior-Senior Prom, and numerous club-sponsored dances. The mid '50s dance styles were dominated by the Bop, Jitterbug, and square dancing. By the mid '60s, these dances were replaced with the Twist, popularized by Chubby Checker and his hit of the same name, and the Mashed Potato, the Monster Mash, the Hully Gully, and the Watusi. The old-fashioned slow dance remained popular throughout the first ten years of Lee High school and beyond.

Gaining Leadership Skills

Leadership skills were and still are learned from holding offices in various clubs and organizations. One of the purposes of the student council was to create interest in all school activities. Each morning the student council president began the day on the intercom with "May I Have Your Attention Please?" Announcements concerning activities and other important matters followed. The student council handled class elections, erected Christmas trees, and published the school calendar, handbook, and phone directory. In the early years of the school, one interesting event the council hosted was Leap Week, held the last week of February, where the girls could ask their favorite "fellow" for a date.

Lee Day festivities were a huge student council responsibility. A typical Lee Day, on a day designated during football season, began with an assembly and continued through the dance that evening. At the conclusion of the Lee Day assembly and pep rally, Miss Lee High and her attendants were announced. After school a parade down Dexter Avenue (later moved to the Atlanta Highway and Coliseum Boulevard) ensued. Several floats, always one reserved for Miss Lee High and attendants, and numerous decorated cars along with the Lee band created a treat for spectators. The climax of Lee Day came during the halftime intermission of the football game when Miss Lee High and attendants were introduced to Montgomery football fans. The day's celebration concluded with a dance following the game at the YMCA (1955) or at the school.

Another opportunity for leadership and activities was found in the yearbook. In the first few years, Lee's *Scabbard* staff won top honors in a statewide contest for high school yearbooks at the University of Alabama. The very first *Scabbard* took sweepstakes honors as the best in the state. This honor continued to be won by Lee for several years. Some 90 percent of students purchased a yearbook, quite a tribute to the efforts of the impressive *Scabbard* staffs.

The *Stars and Bars*, the excellent school newspaper was also begun in 1955–56. Anyone wanting to know what high school life was like could get a pretty clear picture just from reading the *Stars and Bars*. One knew what songs were the most popular, what movies were liked by the high school crowd, and who the best athletes were.

Popular Entertainment

In the 1950s, rock 'n' roll took Lee High School and America by storm. Elvis Presley had top hits such as "Heartbreak Hotel," "Don't be Cruel," "Hound Dog," and "Love Me Tender," to name a few. The Everly Brothers ("Bird Dog" and "Devoted to You"), The Platters ("The Great Pretender"), Little Richard ("Long Tall Sally"), Big Bopper ("Chantilly Lace") and many others made the music of the '50s popular with the Lee students. Some classics stayed popular, such as Doris Day's "Whatever Will Be Will Be (Que Sera Sera)"and Pat Boone's "I Almost Lost My Mind," "Friendly Persuasion," and "I'll Be Home."

By the mid '60s, students favored the Temptations, Sonny and Cher, the Beach Boys, and the English groups—the Beatles, Gerry and the Pacemakers, and Herman's Hermits, to name a few. Students enjoyed the sounds of these popular artists hour upon hour on radio stations WAPX, WBAM, and WHHY. Most students tuned in early upon waking and again as soon as school was out. Don Davis ('58) writes: "Life changed when I got my job at the A&P and bought a 1948 Buick Tudor. I had wheels and freedom to come and go. Most of my female passengers were in need of a ride with no interest in me. We would sit in the car and run the battery down listening to the radio every morning. To go home, I would push the straight shift in neutral, push down as hard as I could, jump in, put it in second gear, pop the clutch and be on my way, trailing a curl of oily smoke."

Musicals were a popular movie type during the first ten years of Lee High

School. The '50s ushered in *Oklahoma*, followed by blockbusters *My Fair Lady*, *Mary Poppins*, and *The Sound of Music*. Favorite movies of this period included lots of beach movies, such as *Where the Boys Are* and *Gidget*. *April Love*, *A Summer Place*, *Bye, Bye Birdie*, *A Hard Day's Night*, and *Splendor in the Grass* were all popular with Lee teens. The Paramount and Empire theaters, as well as the Montgomery Drive-In, were popular venues. Often times, couples would pull up on Watson Circle alongside the drive-in and watch the movie from the roadside, straining to hear the sound from the nearest speakers on the drive-in lot. Now that's what you call a cheap date!

Another form of entertainment in the 1950s, relatively new to high schoolers, was TV. "The Jack Benny Show," "The Ed Sullivan Show," "I love Lucy," "Leave It to Beaver," "Gunsmoke," " Dobie Gillis," " Have Gun Will Travel," "The Rifleman," "Make Room for Daddy," "Wagon Train," "77 Sunset Strip," "Alfred Hitchcock," "Father Knows Best," and "Perry Mason" topped the popular list.

Fashions

A highlight in the life of a senior girl, whether it was 1956 or 1965, was the anticipation of graduation and attending all the teas for fellow graduates. According to the *Stars and Bars*, every girl at Lee attended at least one tea in May. These teas honoring graduates-to-be were quite the social gatherings. What to wear became a pressing issue. In May 1956, many girls chose cool summer cotton prints with low necklines and full skirts. Cummerbunds were in style this season also. Pastel-colored or white barefoot sandals were popular with this style dress. Another dress popular this season was the slim sheath in exotic colors, copied from the Oriental style. The LHS graduation crowd was definitely in style.

Boys in 1956 also took the fashion spotlight with orlon and wool V-neck sweaters and flashy plaid cotton shirts. Matching shirts and socks were hitting the fashion scene also. Girls went from bobbie socks to bare legs between 1955 and 1965, while boys traded white socks for colored "Gold Cup" socks or no socks at all. By 1965 the saddle oxford had been replaced with flats or the penny loafer, especially the Weejun brand for those who could afford it. Girls wore full skirts with layers of net petticoats beneath in 1955, but the '60s girls favored the A-line skirt and tailored dresses. The shirtwaist dress remained a staple in the wardrobe, but the skirt was now A-line. Ten years made quite a difference in fashion as usual.

Spring Break and Off-Campus Activities

Activities during AEA spring holidays were gaily anticipated. Planning for a glorious weekend was the topic of many lively conversations during the month prior to the March holiday. Florida seemed to be the most popular destination. The most frequented places in Panama City were the Hangout, Aultman's, Jenkins, the Y, and carpet golf courses, according to the *Stars and Bars*.

Off-campus activities in the "Fabulous Fifties" centered around drive-in restaurants. According to Walt Boswell ('56) in his essay "Cruising the Drive-in Culture," the drive-in restaurant was "the center of all that was holy to a teenager—a cherished asphalt Mecca where young people met to swap stories about fading romances, the 'grooviest' rock and roll stars, the 'hottest' girls, the 'coolest' guys, the 'fastest' wheels, the 'nastiest looking' teachers, and the 'squarest' parents."

Boswell goes on to cite the four most influential drive-ins to teens in the fifties in Montgomery as the Parkmore at 3036 Mt. Meigs Road (Atlanta Highway today), Susie's Drive-in on Fairview Avenue, Cordell's at Mt Meigs Road and Coliseum Boulevard, and Paul's Sugar and Spice, a block north of the Coliseum at the corner of Federal Drive and Coliseum Boulevard. He says the Sugar and Spice was "probably the most popular teenage hangout in the city, at least throughout the late fifties."

As Boswell recalls, ". . .most of my friends went to Paul's place to flirt with the carhops, as best we knew how; talk to 'nice' girls, whenever we could work up the nerve; and try to look as 'cool' as Elvis in our turned up collars and ducktail haircuts. . .Of course the 'nice' girls called us 'hoods,' but we didn't really care what they called us. The idea was to look as much like James Dean in *Rebel without a Cause* as we possibly could."

A night at Sugar and Spice might go something like this: "After making several turns around the drive-in parking lot in low gear . . . the really 'cool' guy would park his 'wheels' in a very conspicuous place, flash his lights once or twice, and then wait the necessary five minutes or so until one of Paul's gum-smacking carhops finally made it out to where 'Mr. Wonderful' sat in all his teenage glory . . . the typical 'cool' guy would order a 'cherry coke' and if he were really 'loaded,' a 'boat' of French fries and a tenderloin sandwich."

Bill Cordell's place, at the opposite end of Coliseum Boulevard from Sugar and Spice, was famous for the best fried chicken in Montgomery. Boswell said, "Even parents agreed that Cordell's was one of the best all-around restaurants in town. In fact, that's probably what brought Bill's place down in the long run. It was just a little too popular with our, parents, if you know what I mean."

"In general, the toughest kids in town hung out at Susie's or the Hollywood Drive-in on Bell Street. As I recall, some of them went to these places just to prove how 'tough' they really were. In fact, the rumor was that there was actually a list floating around that 'ranked' these 'tough' guys according to the number of fistfights they had won against other 'ranked contenders.'"

Cruising the highway remained popular during the first ten years of Lee High School's existence. As Walt Boswell put it ". . . no matter what you drove, where you went, or what you did when you got there, you almost always wound up back at Paul's Sugar and Spice—or some place like it—where you cruised round and round the blacktop until there was nothing left to see." The names of the drive-ins may have changed over these ten years, but the mission remained the same . . . to enjoy the "Happy Days" and nights.

But, as Jim Vickrey reminded us, other students bypassed both the drive-ins and most Lee extra-curricular activities because they had part-time or near full-time jobs or they were pursuing excellence in personal hobbies. An example of the latter is Laurens Pierce, a long-time Montgomery auto executive who wrote up the following account at Vickrey's request:

> Why did I not take time to have my senior picture taken for the 1960 Lee Annual, or to participate in any of the school activities during my three years at Lee? I was devoting 100 percent of my spare time and energy to become one of the very best model airplane flyers in the country, and it paid off.
>
> I started flying model airplanes when I was 10 years old—the result

of my Sunday School teacher's introducing me to the hobby one Sunday afternoon in 1952. As the years passed, I was fortunate to work after school at several of Montgomery's great "Hobby Shops," where I made many friends and contacts who mentored me into the model airplane world, introducing me to products and parts, original engines and fuels, and experience and knowledge needed to achieve my ambitious goals.

As a result, in 1956, 1957, 1958, and yet again in 1959, I won the overall Alabama State "Junior" Model Airplane Championship, thereby qualifying to compete in the National and International World Model Airplane Championships. Accordingly, in 1957 I won 2nd place in International Combat at the International World Championships in Miami—the equivalent of an Olympic Silver Medal. In 1959 I won 1st place in Class "A" Speed and 2nd place in Class "B" Speed—the equivalent of Gold and Silver Medals. During that extraordinary period of success, I benefited from custom-made engines and racing fuels and custom-made model planes that enabled me to fly "mono" rather than with the "dual" line other competitors had been tied to—and to do so within a week of its being introduced to the entire model world!

And that's what I was doing and where I was from 1957 to 1960, while other Lee students were engaging in more typical high school extracurricular activities . . .

8

Athletics: 'A Pattern for Greatness'

By Ed Jones

The Beginning, 1955–56

In the spring of 1955, a new high school was being born on Ann Street in what was then East Montgomery. At the time, Sidney Lanier High School, which had been an intellectual bastion of excellence and an athletic power in the state of Alabama, was bulging at the seams, with over 2,000 students. News of the new school's birth was somewhat confusing to nineteen Lanier football players who would be eligible to transfer to the new school, which would be named Robert E. Lee High School. They had

Lee High's first football brain trust: from left, Jim Chafin, Pete Lee, Tom Jones, and Leon Ford.

Former Lanier players who made up the nucleus of the first Lee football team included: (front, from left) Billy McNair, T; Charles Tatum, E; James Johnson, G; Judson Huett, G; Charles Brophy, G; Durden Lee, C; Pat Garner, E; (back, from left) Ed Jones, QB/HB; Jackie Spencer, HB; Ed Spencer, HB; Mickey Newman, FB; Cliff Little, QB; Earl Mills, HB. Not pictured: Raymond Parker, G, and Rex Akin, T.

all grown up hoping to play football at Lanier, so there was some hesitation as to what to do.

Some fellow by the name of Tom Jones had been hired by the Board of Education to be the head football coach. Frankly, none of the players had ever heard of Coach Tom Jones. However, he had been a very successful coach at Hayneville High School, a 1-A school in the then-3A classification system in Alabama. There he coached outstanding players like QB Mac Champion, HB Wilber Supple, and FB Pete Lee. It would not be long before every football fan in Alabama would be familiar with the name of Tom Jones. (He passed away in the summer of 2014 at the age of 90, before he could be interviewed specifically for this book. A great offensive mind is gone, but his influence remains.)

Most of the guys had heard little about the new school. Some thought that it might be a small military school. Coach Neal Posey, the Lanier basketball coach had been named athletic director at Lee. Coach Posey called for a meeting of all Lanier football players that lived in the new school district that would serve Lee High School. That only involved nineteen players who were upcoming juniors and seniors. They had the choice to transfer or stay at Lanier.

Our meeting with Coach Posey was held in the Lanier gymnasium in the spring of 1955. He told us that Coach Jim Chafin, the first-year line coach at Lanier would be going to Lee also to coach the line and be the baseball coach. Coach Chafin was well liked by the players. Posey did an excellent job of convincing the guys that Robert E. Lee would be a first-class school and would have a first-class football program. He said that the senior class would be allowed to pick the colors, the nickname, the name of the yearbook and the name of the school newspaper. He said that Coach Tom Jones wanted the colors to be dark red and white so that the offense could hide the ball better. All but four players agreed to transfer.

Football

So, in the spring of 1955, 15 "former" Lanier players put on brand new practice uniforms of the Robert E. Lee Generals. They met their new head coach for the first time in the dressing room at Capitol Heights Junior High School where most had played junior high ball under Coach Kyle Renfroe. Renfroe had wanted the Lee job but ultimately decided to continue coaching at Capitol Heights; however, he was very helpful to the new Lee coaching staff.

Only one of the players that transferred was a starter at Lanier: All-State left halfback Earl Mills. He would make All-American at Lee.

The Lee field was still under construction so the spring practices were held at nearby Capitol Heights. There was no grass and the practice field was littered with cinders. There were lots of cinder cuts and skinned elbows that spring. The team would first set foot on the Lee practice field in August of 1955.

Incoming sophomores from Capitol Heights helped, especially fullback Carl Hopson and center Billy Williams. Coach Jones now had seventeen players. Other transferring Lanier students who had not played football at Lanier but came out for the Lee team included Eely Jackson, Jack Bell, "Smokey" Evans, Benny Meadows, Richard Jordan, and Joe McDonald. Overall, the team had enough depth for Coach Jones to record a 6–4 season that fall playing a "big boy" schedule. The only losses were to Ramsey,

Phillips, Fairfield, and Opelika.

Jones would only lose nine more times in the next ten years on the way to five state championships. That first team accounted for a third of his total losses at Lee. But the foundation had been laid!

Due to a broken nose, senior halfback Earl Mills wore the first face mask in the history of Robert E. Lee football. Sophomore fullback Carl Hopson scored the first Lee touchdown in the opening 1955 game against Prattville.

Coach Jones, who played for the great "Hot" O'Brien at Tallassee, took over the duties of athletic director from Posey, who had taken a job outside of coaching. Someone had to replace Posey as basketball coach. Coach Leon Ford was picked for that job along with the duties of coaching the ends in football. Coach George Peters was selected to coach the "B" Team.

Tom Jones was known for his quick, fast offenses throughout a magnificent high school coaching career: 139 wins, 28 losses, 13 ties over 18 years—an 80.8 winning percentage. His record in seven years at Hayneville HS had been 46–16–8, a 71.4 winning percentage. At Lee, his record was even more impressive: 93–12–5, for an 86.8 winning percentage. To put this into perspective, consider that any football coach at any level who wins 68 percent of his games is considered a great coach. Very few in the history of the game at any level have won 86 percent of their games at one school.

After the '67 season, Coach Ralph "Shug" Jordan hired Tom Jones as his offensive coach. Auburn had lost five straight games to Alabama. Tom did a good job with each freshman class and recruited some excellent players to Auburn. His most famous class was the 1968 class that included a guy named Pat Sullivan and a guy named Terry Beasley, who was a Lee alumnus. Tom might have taught him a thing or two, you think? Auburn beat Alabama in '69, '70 and '72.

CHAPLAIN LOUIS ARMSTRONG

The November 10, 1955, *Stars and Bars* noted that the Rev. Louis Armstrong, pastor of Morningview Baptist Church since its inception in 1949, had been chosen as the official chaplain of the football team. The article reported that Armstrong "has shown his support by attending all football games, at home and on the road. He has been at many of the practices in the afternoons and has always shown interest in all the boys on the team."

Armstrong had served four years in the Army Chaplain Corps, including three years overseas in General Douglas McArthur's Far East Command Headquarters. In Montgomery, he was active in community organizations and recognized for his service to youth throughout the city.

Rev. Armstrong was a close friend of Tim Carlton and the Lee coaches, particularly Jim Chafin, who attended Morningview Baptist. His son, "Chip" (now Dr. Louis Armstrong), was the student trainer for Lee's athletic department.

Chip recalls receiving a phone call one Saturday night when his father was not at home. A lady wanted to say she had seen a photo in the newspaper with Rev. Armstrong waving a towel amid the Lee coaching staff on the sidelines of a football game played the previous evening at Cramton Bowl. She took offense that a minister would engage in such activities. Chip asked her if she knew where her own pastor was or what he was doing on Friday night. "No," she answered. "Well," said Chip, "everyone in Montgomery knows where my Dad was and what he was doing."

Sometimes, perhaps, he could be too close to the action, as recalled by Charles Smith ('61, who played football and ran track at Lee and later lettered in track at Auburn): "We were over in Selma playing A. G. Parrish High School. We fell behind and as we all gathered in the dressing room at halftime, you could have heard a pin drop. We were waiting anxiously for Coach Jones to light into us. He finally appeared in the doorway of the cramped visitors' dressing room. He stared us down and, without a word being spoken, he looked to his right and kicked a full water-bucket that he saw there (it was probably planted). Then he turned and stormed out, not realizing that when he kicked that old bucket, its entire contents had landed upon Chaplain Armstrong, making him look like the winning coach at the end of a game after he'd been drenched by happy players with Gatorade. It was one of the funniest things I'd ever seen, but I was not about to laugh and neither was anyone else present. But we went back out on the field of play and romped over the Parrish Partisans."

Basketball

Coach Leon Ford tried to round up as many football players as he could to supplement the depth of his first Lee basketball team. Cliff Little, Bill McNair, Ed Spencer, Jackie Spencer, and Eely Jackson answered the call. Walter Cooper, Don Crocker, Bill Shepherd, Wayne Graydon, and Ken Kransusch made up the rest of the varsity.

Coach Ford really had a job in front of him. The tallest man on the team was Bill McNair at 6–3. So rebounding would have to come from everybody on the squad. There was no individual star of that first team. Sophomore Don Crocker was the most talented basketball player, but, he had just come over from Capitol Heights Junior High School. Bill McNair did most of the heavy work under the basket, which gave him opportunities to score, and he did. Senior Bill Shepherd was a natural athlete who did most of the ball handling along with senior Ed Spencer. Cliff Little was a good shooter along with Wayne Graydon and Ken Kransusch. Eely Jackson, Walter Cooper and Jackie Spencer provided excellent depth at several positions. Coach Ford led this undersized and scrappy team to a 14–6 record in the first year.

Baseball

The first Lee baseball team won 9 and lost 4, highlighted by two wins over Lanier (first, a 10–1 shellacking of the veteran Poets, then a much closer 4–3 win; southpaw Wayne Graydon pitched both games). Also, the Generals beat Selma twice, 9–0 and 6–0.

Coach Jim Chafin had the Generals ready to play, and play they did, winning the County Championship. The first win ever was against Ramer. The first loss was at the hands of the Auburn University freshman team, an over-match for sure.

Bill Shepherd collected the first hit in Lee High history against Ramer. Bill McNair scored Lee's first run in the same game. Wayne Graydon, Johnny Andrews, and Don Sellers made up an excellent pitching rotation. Lee LaFollette, James Parham and Bill McNair provided power. The infield of Charles Brophy (C), Walter Cooper (3B), Bill Shepherd (SS), Eely Jackson (2B), and Lee LaFollette (1B) made it difficult for the opposition to get a ball past the infield. Graydon, Jackson, and Shepherd were among several

Generals who went on to play freshman baseball at Auburn.

A distinction of Lee's first baseball team is that they were the first team to beat Lanier in any sport. Every team following would have to break records established by this team.

Track

Coach Tom Jones was officially the track coach. However, several volunteers with track experience helped in organizing the events and teaching proper techniques. Also, there were a few experienced runners and field men who had already lettered in track at Lanier, including sprinter Ed Spencer and pole vaulter Benny Meadows. Meadows had placed second in the pole vault in the '55 state meet. Eely Jackson was the number two pole vaulter. Pat Garner was the discus thrower (he later threw the discus at Troy State College).

The 440-yard relay was made up of Carl Hopson, Jackie Spencer, Charles Tatum, and Ed Spencer, in that order. In the 880 relay were Hopson, Tatum, Don Hunt, and Ed Spencer. The mile relay was made up of Jackie Spencer, Craig Miller, Jackie Bryant, and Ed Morelock. The sprint medley relay was run by Morelock, Hunt, Tatum, and Joe McDonald. Meadows, Garner and Larry Sanders were the high jumpers. Ed Spencer and Bryant participated in the broad jump.

Lee did very well in the 440 relay and was competitive in the other relays. Meadows again placed in the pole vault at the state meet. Ed Spencer placed in the 100-yard dash. Ed Spencer and Hunt ran the 220-yard dash.

Being the first year of track at Lee, there were not many participants. Even so, they did very well. Things looked good for the second year. Lee would lose only Ed Spencer, Tatum, Meadows, Garner, and Jackson.

1956–57

Football

Robert E. Lee's second team was a harbinger to the future. Coach Tom Jones finally had what he wanted, speed at the right positions and quickness at the others. Quarterback Cliff Little had a year of experience behind him and had improved his passing skills. He had targets like ends Jack Bell, Joe McDonald, John Livings, and Freddie Black. Halfbacks Jackie Spencer, Larry Curry, Donald Hunt, and Jackie Bryant were probably the four fastest white backs in the state. Fullback Carl Hopson was developing into the best running back in the state. "Smokey" Evans (T), Rex Akin (T), Neal Rucker (G), James Johnson (G), Billy Williams (C), "Skeeter" Gunn (G), and Bill Vinson (QB) developed into tough and talented defensive players. (Spencer would receive a full scholarship to Auburn, where he won the Mississippi State game in 1959 with a 60-yard punt return. Little was signed by Wake Forest where he excelled at defensive back. Bell played at Baylor.)

The '56 team started a trend of undefeated teams that would continue through the 1970s. The 1956 Generals rolled through Winfield, Auburn, Troy, B. B. Comer, Selma, Alex City, Opelika, Tallassee, Dothan, and U.M.S. for a 10–0 record. The only close game was Troy, 14–12. The Generals outscored the opposition, 329–65 in one of the most dominating performances of any Lee High football team.

Basketball

As in football, Coach Leon Ford had a little more to work with in his second year as the General's basketball coach. Jackie Spencer, Ken Kransuzch, Bobby Sandlin, Don Crocker, Ed Morelock, and Cliff Little had gained valuable experience in Lee's debut season. This year they were joined by many other sophomores and juniors who were able to get good playing time with blowouts over Holtville, Clanton, Tuscaloosa, Wetumpka and Ramer on the way to an overall record of 13–5. Basketball at Lee was now a good spectator sport that would get the Generals ready to take on Lanier the next year, something that everyone in East Montgomery was looking forward to.

Baseball

Coach Chafin's second Lee baseball team was a good mixture of players off the football and basketball teams. The baseball-only exceptions were Lester Henderson (3B), James Parham (SS), John Dunbar (2B), and Mickey McNight (C), who made up an infield that was the backbone of the team. In the outfield, Bill Vinson, John Moore, Alan Wilson, and Juddy Smith were ballhawks. The pitching duties went to two lefthanders, Don Sellers and Jimmy Crysel. Dickie Hanna was the right-handed ace. This squad accomplished much and will go down as one of Coach Chafin's best.

Track

Coach Leon Ford took over as track coach in the spring of 1956. The sprinters were Don Hunt, Carl Hopson, Craig Miller, Bart Kennedy, and John Moore. Dickie Hanna and Trey Causey handled the broad and high jumps. Billy Wilkes and Leon Darby did the heavy lifting. Ed Morelock ran the middle distances along with Bobby Moore. Other contributors were Earl Young, Sammy Davenport, Billy Holley, Charles Pritchard, Jerry Calloway, Danny Rushton, Larry Sanders, David Dillard, Paul Ohme, Gerald Anderson, and James Johnson.

Wrestling

Coach Tom Jones thought that a wrestling team might benefit his football program, so he organized the first Lee wrestling team, a sport Lee would excel at in coming years. Some of the football players came out for the team, including Charles Tatum, Neal Rucker, "Smokey" Evans, Judson Huett, "Skeeter" Gunn, James Johnson, Charlie Jones, and "Juddy" Smith. This conglomeration of athletes was totally new to wrestling. Courage and the desire to win, which they learned in other sports, powered the Generals to a second-place finish in the state tournament. The best wrestler in this group was sophomore "Skeeter" Gunn. He was hard to beat in the 138-pound classification. Even though the season was short it ended well and established a precedent for future teams.

1957–58

Football

Football at Robert E. Lee under Coach Tom Jones had become big time by the fall of 1957. The Lee-Lanier game would be held for the first time at the end of the season. The much anticipated game kept the excitement going all fall. Coach Pete Lee, who had played for Coach Jones at Hayneville, had

Richard Jordan—an outstanding player on the 1957 team. His generosity made this book possible.

joined the Lee coaching staff (and was a future head coach himself). The third edition of the Generals was probably the best yet even though their record would not indicate this. After bowling over Greenville, Tallassee, Troy and B. B. Comer, the big red machine lost a heartbreaker in Selma. Lee then dispensed with Alex City, Opelika and Ramsey. A tie with Dothan could possibly be explained by anticipation of the next week's game against the Poets of Lanier, when the Generals came up short before 25,000 watchers at Cramton Bowl. Lee was leading 12–7 late in the fourth quarter when Lanier quarterback Tommy Sewell broke the hearts of all Lee players, fans and coaches. Sewell dashed for a short touchdown to give Lanier the win 14–12. The greatest rivalry in high school football had begun.

Fullback Carl Hopson had become one of the most prolific runners among Alabama's white high schools. He would later play at the University of Alabama in the first recruiting class of Coach Paul "Bear" Bryant. Halfback Jackie Bryant provided speed to the outside, taking pitchouts from quarterback Bart Kennedy. Billy Williams anchored the line and started at linebacker. Leon Darby and Williams were also excellent centers. Williams and Hopson were the linebackers. John Livings and Dickie Hanna held down each end. Billy Dupree was a tiger on the defensive line. The 1957 record of 7–2–1 was a big disappointment for such a talented squad.

BASKETBALL

Coach Leon Ford's third basketball team was one of his best and played Lee's toughest schedule up to this point. Center Reese Carr handled the rebounding and the putbacks. Star forward Don Crocker was a big scorer with his jump shots. Alan Wilson, Billy Dupree, and Bill Dobbins were tough rebounders. Most of the ball handling was taken care of by Bart Kennedy and Jerry Chafin. Paul Ohme, Hudson Courtney, and Donny Tucker played key roles as well. Lee basketball was now on par with the perennial powers Sidney Lanier, Murphy, Tuscaloosa, Eufaula, and the big schools in Birmingham. The Generals beat Tuscaloosa and Winfield and split with Sidney Lanier, Vigor, and Selma on the way to a 15–7 record.

BASEBALL

Once again the Lee baseball team had an excellent infield in catcher Mickey McKnight, third baseman Lester Henderson, shortstop James Parham, second baseman Bart Kennedy, and first baseman Louis Surles. The outfield was covered by John Dunbar, Fred Cauthen, Juddy Smith, John Moore, and Frank Gibbons. Left-handers Don Sellers and Jimmy Crysel led the pitching rotation along with sophomore righthander Rodney Bell and junior righthander John Andrews.

Coach Pete Lee assisted Coach Jim Chafin for the first time. He was the designated tobacco chewer. The '58 squad defeated Alex City twice, Prattville, LaFayette, and Ramer to get the Generals off to a 5–0 start. The drive for an undefeated season was stopped by Selma, 5–2. Another win against Ramer followed. Taking a 5–1 record into the Lanier game gave the

Generals hope, but the Poets snuffed that out with a 7–3 win. In a return game, the Po ets won again, 4–1. However, the season ended on a positive note as the Generals made up for that first loss of the season by defeating Selma 9–8 in 14 innings.

Coach Chafin completed his third-straight winning season on the diamond. But even better times were yet to come.

Track

There happened to be a lot of speed on Lee's outstanding 1957 football team. That bode well for Coach Leon Ford's 1958 track team.

The sprints were run by fullback Carl Hopson and halfback Jackie Bryant, along with sophomores Bill Goodwin and Ben Wood who had been on the "B" team in the fall. Dickie Hanna and Bill Holley joined this group for the sprint relays. Hanna also participated in the high jump and the broad jump. On the discus and shot put, Tad Bowman, Allen James, John Smith, and David Christian did the heavy work. Sophomore Harry Hydrick was used in various events because of his versatility. He would later become an excellent runner. Other members of the team who contributed to a successful season were Billy Roy, Earl Young, Bill Goodwin, Wayne Bozeman, Kenneth Dickey, Jimmy Hall, Errol Vick, David Stroud, Gerald Anderson, David Dillard, Larry Sanders, Charles Pricket, Buddy Smith, Phil Thompson, James Hufman, and Jerry Callaway.

1958–59

Football

The fourth edition of the Lee football team will be remembered for several firsts. Most important was the first win over crosstown rival Lanier, 26–19. Almost as important was the Class AAA football state championship. Coach Tom Jones's second undefeated team in four years rolled over Greenville, Tallassee, Anniston, Phillips, Selma, and Alex City. Then wins in the last four weeks of the season over Woodlawn, Ramsey, Dothan, and the big one over Lanier propelled the Generals to their first of many state championships.

Quarterback Bart Kennedy was magnificent running the option play. His deceptive ball handling kept opponents guessing all year. Kennedy won All-City, All-Conference, All-State, and All-Southern honors for his stellar play in his senior year. Senior center Leon Darby and senior guard Earl Brophy were also named to the All-City, All-Conference, and All-State teams. Senior halfbacks Hulon Neese and John Moore, along with an excellent corps of junior backs, made Lee's one of the most talented group of running backs in the state. Rodney Bell, Ben Wood, and Bill Goodwin provided Lee with speed unmatched by any other team in the state. Senior guard Billy Wilkes and senior tackle Kent Kelso opened lots of holes for the fleet backs.

Senior tackles James Sexton, Greg Guthrie, and All-State Dudley Gordon, along with senior guard Pookie Arnold, anchored the Big Red line. All-City linebacker Craig Hopson, a junior, along with ends Jerry Moreland, Jimmy Crysel, Reese Carr, and Trey Causey played outstanding as well. Moreland made an unbelievable catch to help Lee beat Lanier and preserve the 10–0 record.

Although the Generals would win many state football championships, the 1958 team was one of the best in Lee history.

Basketball

Coach Leon Ford had been building his basketball program for three years. The 1958–59 squad reflected the results of that work, with twenty-three wins and only seven losses on the way to the championship of the Confederate Conference, first place in the Third District of the Alabama High School Association, and third place in the AHSA state tournament in Tuscaloosa.

Junior center Reese Carr used his 6'5" height to control the backboards leading a great front line that was hard to penetrate. Trey Causey, a 6'3" forward, added more height to the squad. Forwards Jerry Moreland, Alex Moseley, Paul Ohme, and Hudson Courtney were all over six feet, which gave Coach Ford a lot of choices.

The backcourt was handled by Bart Kennedy, Donny Tucker, and Frank Gibbons. Kennedy was the "quarterback" of the offense. His superb ball handling kept defenses from being successful with the press.

Other Lee teams in later years would be compared to this outstanding basketball team. Coach Ford had produced good teams before but this team had been his finest, finishing 23–7.

Weightlifting

This year a Lee teacher who was a serious weightlifter decided to start a team for the sport. "Coach" Jerry Windsor already knew some of the students who were interested. Bob Bedsole and Leon Darby were active weightlifters at the time. They talked to fellow football players Tad Bowman and Greg Guthrie about joining the team. They in turn talked to other students who were interested. Soon "Coach" Windsor had cobbled together a team. Wade Johnson, Donnie James, Larry Vann, Wayne Bozeman, and John Smith were also on the team. Meets were held at YMCAs and health clubs. There were local, state, and regional meets.

The events were broken down in weight classes. Each weight class had minimum lifts to qualify each lifter. All classes participated in three lifts. The military press was done with the weight held at shoulder height, then pushed bar straight above the head and held for two seconds. This required tremendous arm and shoulder strength. All the lifts required a strong back because the end position would have the lifter standing with the weights causing much strain on the back muscles. The snatch was the second lift, requiring the lifter to take the bar from floor to an overhead position in one movement. The third lift was the clean and jerk. This started similar to the snatch but the bar would be brought from the floor to a resting position at shoulder-width stance to a split-leg stance which allowed an assist of momentum as the lifter got under the bar and held it straight above the head.

Baseball

This team was Coach Chafin's fourth-straight winning squad. Catcher Mickey McNight and infielder Bart Kennedy led the Generals to a 9–5 record, beating Lanier twice, 5–4 and 2–0. The Howard College freshman team gave Lee two of the five losses. McNight was flawless, leading the team from his catcher position. He was lethal with his bat as well. The infield was tight with Bart Kennedy, Rodney Bell, Bill Hydrick, and John

Coach Jim Chafin, one of the best baseball coaches then in Alabama, instructs Wayne Conner as Jim Kwater watches.

Moore providing the leadership. First baseman Reese Carr used his height to snatch every throw. Don Phillips provided excellent backup at catcher for McNight. John David Ramsey, Alec Moseley, Frank Gibbons, and Jack Lang roamed the outfield.

Coach Chafin had five pitchers to choose from. Jimmy Crysel, the only left-hander, got most of the work. Bert Estes, Jimmy Forsythe, and Leonard Hall performed well also.

Lee defeated Clanton, Enterprise, Selma, Alex City, and B. B. Comer, losing only 8–7 to Selma in the first half of the season. They took care of

Selma, 5–0, avenging their first loss of the season. But for that one-run loss, the Generals would have been undefeated going into the first game with the Howard freshman. Lee went on to win four of its last seven games. The victims were Clanton, Alex City, Lanier twice, and B. B. Comer. However, the season ended on a sour note as Lee lost their last two games to the Howard freshman and the last game to Selma, against whom they were 1–2 on the season.

Track

Coach Pete Lee was a hard taskmaster in a rebuilding year for Lee track. The team lacked the speed of other track squads at Lee. However, this team was strong in the field events, giving the Generals a good season. Buddy Smith won first place in the state as Lee's number one pole vaulter. Warren Hardy placed in the shot put.

Bob Ritter showed great promise in the sprints and the middle distances. Allen James did well in the shot put and the discus. Mason Wood excelled in most of the running events. Jim Hall showed well in the distance runs.

1959–60

Football

Coach Tom Jones led his Generals to their second-straight Class AAA state championship, making Robert E. Lee the top football program among Alabama's white high schools. Co-captains Allen James, Ben Wood, and Craig Hopson led the team to an 8–0 record through October, extending their winning streak to 16 games. They had handled Greenville, Tallassee, Anniston, and Phillips with ease. Then came a tough 13–7 win over Selma. Alex City, Dothan, and Woodlawn next fell before the Big Red Machine. Then came the Lanier Poets. Before a capacity crowd of 25,000 screaming fans. Lee was trailing 7–6 in the third quarter when Lanier blocked a punt and recovered it in the Lee end zone to go up 14–6. This broke the Generals' back and the 16-game winning streak.

Even so, Lee maintained its lofty ranking in the state, with a chance to still win the state championship. A win over Ramsey in the last game of

Glen Gilley makes a move on rival Lanier.

the season would help put the Generals over the top again. Trailing 13–7 late in the fourth quarter, Lee got the break it needed. Junior tackle Wayne Caine recovered a Ramsey fumble and Lee was back in business in Ramsey territory. The not-to-be-denied running of Ben Wood, Rodney Bell, and sophomore halfback Wayne Beasley put the ball on the one-yard line. Fullback Ben Wood smashed over to tie the game. Then Wood calmly kicked the extra point to put Lee ahead for good. However, the last minute kept all 20,000 fans on their feet. Ramsey took the kick-off and drove 70 yards to the Lee 10. With six seconds remaining, Ramsey called time out and lined up for the winning field goal. It was not to be. Defensive end Reese Carr used all of his height to block the kick. Thus ended one of the most exciting games ever played in the state. The win also impressed the voters enough to put the Generals on top for the second straight year – and the third time in four years. A dynasty was forming!

Basketball

Coach Leon Ford had been building for a basketball season like this one.

His team went 25–6, beating Lanier three times, on the way to the most successful season in Lee history so far. Guards Jimmy Forsythe and Ware Tatum were the ball handlers that kept Lee away from many turnovers. Forwards James Warr, Bill Boyd, Bert Estes and Charles Anderson were good shooters as well as good rebounders. Center Reese Carr used his 6'5" height to control the backboard and score under the basket. And score they did. They scored 80 points against Prattville, and 79 points against Escambia, 77 points against Alex City, 76 points against Winfield and Central, 75 points against Maplesville, 72 points against Murphy and 70 against Clanton. Most of the teams in that era were scoring in the fifties.

This squad beat Lanier twice, 52–46 and 50–39. That was the lowest point total of the year for the Poets. The only losses were to Fayette, Selma, Alex City, Tuscaloosa and twice to nemesis Eufaula. However in the first half of the season, Lee defeated Eufaula for the first time in history, 52–41.

It would be a long time before a Lee team would score as had the 1959–60 Generals. The Generals started the season 15–0. Selma broke the spell with a one point win, 35–34. Reese Carr won nearly every available award, including All-state and Mr. Basketball, and Lee finished with a 25–6 record.

Baseball

Coach Jim Chafin was fast becoming one of the best baseball coaches in the state as well as being the best football line coach in the state. The 1960 squad won over Tuscaloosa County, Tuscaloosa, Selma, Opelika, and twice over Catholic on the way to a 6–0 start. A 5–2 loss to Clanton in the seventh game started a discouraging slide. Then followed another win over Opelika, 6–2. The Generals were still rolling along with an outstanding Then the bottom fell out. A 3–2 loss to Phenix City was followed by two one-run losses to the Lanier Poets, 1–0 and 7–6.

Lee got good pitching from Jimmy Forsythe and Jimmy Crysel. The infield of Donnie Phillips at catcher, Rodney Bell at shortstop, and Reese Carr at first base was tight. Third base and second base were handled by Donnie James, Bill Hydrick, and Leonard Hall. Roaming the outfield was Larry Morris, Jimmy Hobson, Frank Rentz, Charles Crysel, and Bert Estes.

With a mere three more runs in the last three games the team could

Lee High's "Dash Men" for 1960: from left, Randy Hall, Wade Currington, Bob Ritter, Harry Hydrik, and James Berry.

have finished better than its disappointing 7–4 record. Still, the 1960 team gave Coach Chafin his fifth-straight winning season.

Track

Coach Pete Lee had his 1960 Track team well trained and in tip top shape. Without the benefit of really outstanding sprinters, Coach Lee kept experimenting with different combinations. The result was a winning track team again for the Generals. In the sprints James Berry, Harry Hydrick, Bob Ritter, Wade Currington and Randy Hall scored well. Ritter and Hydrick gave the Generals a big boost in the high and low hurdles. The 440 relay team was made up of Wade Currington, Randy Hall, Bob Ritter and Harry Hydrick. The mile relay was handled by David Beasley, Randy Hall, Jim Hall and Wade Currington. Ritter, Currington, Hydrick and Randy Hall were quite busy as they led the Generals Saturday after Saturday.

The distance runners were Richard Piel, Herb Florey, Andy Reeves, Jim

Hall, David Beasley, Richard Hill and John Henley. Field events featured Warren Hardy in the shot put and the discus, Jerry Black with the discus, Phil Hodges in the pole vault. Charles Smith and Howard Roberts were also valuable members of the field events section. Andy Reeves was a valuable member of the team. The all-important managers were Donald Cassaras and Rickey Allen. Coach Pete Lee's track teams started taking the same status of the football, basketball and baseball teams.

1960–61

Football

No team had ever won three state championships in a row in Class AAA football until Coaches Tom Jones, Jim Chafin, Leon Ford, and Pete Lee guided the 1960 Generals to this unprecedented accomplishment. Coach Jones's record after six seasons stood at an amazing 51–7–2 with three undefeated teams in that span. At this point in the history of Lee High School football, no Lee football team had lost to a Birmingham school since the inaugural season in 1955.

Lee's third game was a close 13–6 win over Anniston, then a gut wrenching 7–7 tie with Banks, and a tight 14–7 squeeze in the seventh game with Dothan. In the other games the Generals bulldozed the competition including a 47–7 pasting of Lanier, the most dominating victory to date in the Lee-Lanier series. Lee ended the season 9–0–1.

Junior Rennie Mize and senior Ware Tatum shared the quarterback duties. Tatum also returned punts and kickoffs. Mize had the confidence of the coaches as far as guiding the offense, but Tatum was the better runner with several touchdowns of 70 or more yards. Captain Bob Ritter was the most perfect football player as he excelled on offense and defense and was the spiritual leader of this team. He would exhibit these same qualities for four years on the Missouri Tigers football team along with Tatum. Co-captains Ernie Pilgreen and Raymond DePasquale were the physical leaders on the team, playing both offense and defense. Senior ends Bill Boyd and Burton Lenoir added valuable depth on the defense as did senior tackle Billy Porter. Senior Phil Norton was the most versatile lineman playing both center and

Senior forward Larry Morris rebounding against Lanier.

guard on offense and linebacker on defense.

There may never be another period in the history of Alabama high school football to equal the dominance the Lee Generals exhibited during the seasons of 1958–60.

BASKETBALL

The team started out without one of their best returning players, Jimmy Forsythe, who died suddenly before fall practice began. He would have been a good role player on this squad and was missed by all, especially Coach Leon Ford.

However, some other talent was coming off the great previous season. Guards Ware Tatum and Woody Weaver were not only good ball handlers but big enough to provide much-needed help on the boards. Weaver would continue his career as a Huntingdon College Hall of Fame player, while Tatum went on to the University of Missouri on a football scholarship. He was voted captain of the team as well. Weaver was the leading scorer for the Generals. He also pulled in 185 rebounds.

Senior forwards Larry Morris and Bill Boyd were excellent shooters. They got a lot of help from junior Wade Currington who moved around from forward to center. Senior center Bert Estes served as co-captain. His 275 rebounds led the team. His free-throw shooting was the best on the team.

This team was not as talented as the '59–60 year, but they were scrappy and shot well. They compiled a 29–5 record, were District Three champions, and got to the semifinals of the state tournament before losing to Tuscaloosa. They beat Butler 72–62 in the consolation game thereby finishing third in the state. It sounds better if it is said that only two basketball teams in the state were better.

Coach Leon Ford's record for the last two years was 54–11, an 83 percent winning margin. That was not bad for a school where football was king. The season also continued to add to the dominance over Lanier. The Generals beat Lanier twice in the regular season and once in the finals of the district tournament.

Track

Coach Pete Lee had been building his track program by involving athletes from football and basketball as well as the full-time track specialists. The approach began to pay off in 1961. The state championship 440-relay team of Bob Ritter, Randy Hall, Wade Currington, and James Berry led the Generals to a high team finish in the Alabama State High School track meet. In addition to the members of that record-setting relay team, Coach Lee Coach was blessed with other excellent. Johnny and Wayne Beasley were key in providing depth on the sprints and relays. Currington was especially versatile as he ran the relays and the middle distances and was good in the high jump and broad jump. Charles Smith scored well in the pole vault. Hurdlers David Zorich, Bob Ritter, and Johnny Beasley brought in valuable points. The distance and middle distance events were run by Earl Campbell, J. C. Borders, Don Clary, Jimmy Sims, John Jordan, Doug

Smith, and Currington. Walter Warren, Warren Hardy, Charles Couch, and Cecil Foster excelled in the shot put and the discus throw.

Baseball

Coach Jim Chafin's 1961 team was made up of an accumulation of good athletes. Catchers Jack Lange and Rennie Mize kept a tight rein on a very good infield led by shortstop Larry Morris and first baseman Bert Estes, both three-year veterans. The outfield was covered by John David Ramsey, Frank Rentz, and Charles Crysel. A deep pitching corps was made up of Ronnie Godbold, Wayne Sellers, David Smith, and Leonard Hall.

Lee won its first three games over Opelika, Demopolis and Phenix City before losing 3–0 to Tuscaloosa County. The next game with Tuscaloosa had to be called because of darkness with the score tied 6–6. Then Lee whitewashed Lanier 11–0. Two more wins followed before Lee lost a heartbreaker to Selma 3–2. Then Lee beat Clanton 6–4 in a warm-up before the season finale with Lanier. Unfortunately, Lanier outscored the Generals in a thriller, 9–8. This closed out the season with a record of 7–3–1.

1961–62

Football

The Robert E. Lee General football team of 1961 would be known for many things. One was that they came within one point of making it four state championships in a row. Undefeated going into the Lanier game, Lee was fighting for first place again. But, a 14–13 loss in the last game to the Lanier Poets cost Lee an unprecedented fourth straight title. Another thing this team would be known for is the appearance of the famous red helmets. Toward the end of the season Coach Tom Jones dressed his "Big Red Machine" in red helmets for the first time. It was several games before the Lee-Lanier game. Only a tie with Banks in the fourth game of the season marred a perfect record as Lee lined up to play the powerful Lanier Poets. They had mowed down Woodlawn, Tallassee, Anniston, Selma, Tuscaloosa, Dothan, Shades Valley and Ramsey.

The 8–1–1 record kept Lee in the top echelon of football teams in the state. Quarterback Rennie Mize, a starter for the second year, led the Generals to an outstanding season again. Senior fullback Charles Crysel was a classic runner who just bowled over opponents with his slashing running style. His performance in 1961 earned him a football scholarship to the University of Alabama. Coach Paul W. Bryant liked what he saw. Senior halfbacks Wayne Beasley and Buddy Herring complemented Crysel and Mize. There was no drop-off when junior halfback Johnny Beasley entered the game. Senior tackle Alex Johnson was the inspirational leader of the '61 team. His brother Marvin had played on the first Robert E. Lee team in 1955. Alex would continue his football at Howard College. Guard Cecil Foster anchored the offensive and the defensive lines. His senior performance won him a scholarship at Auburn. Senior center Lloyd Kuczmarski and senior tackle Slugger Allison were mainstays on offense and defense. Junior fullback Walter Warren, a 200-pound piledriver, was called on many times to get crucial short yardage.

The 1961 team was certainly one of the best ever. Coach Tom Jones had built a dynasty on Ann Street. The talent on his '61 team was nearly unmatched.

Basketball

This Lee basketball team played a tough schedule. It was also a rebuilding year for Coach Leon Ford. He lost many good players from the year before. Even so, this team accomplished so much. They started 4–0, including a big win over Murphy, before losing 62–46 to Lanier. Later in the season, Lanier won the rematch 88–55. Lee met Lanier for a third time in the Confederate Conference Tournament, coming up short again, 71–53. Lanier had become a state power and would be hard to beat for a few years.

Co-captains Shorty Piel and Wade Currington were the team leaders. Senior forwards David Myrick and Hank Garrett were good shooters. Senior center Miles Hall provided relief for senior center Currington; they were the leading rebounders. Senior guard Warren Oliver and sophomore guard Tommy Gowan helped Piel bring the ball down the court. Lack of depth at guard and forward was a problem all year.

Coach Ford had his seventh-straight winning season. Including tournaments, the Generals won eleven games and lost nine. This was to be Coach Ford's last Lee squad. He was hired at the end of the year by the University of Chattanooga.

BASEBALL

Coach Jim Chafin's team was again one of the best in the area and was rolling along with a 5–1 record when the wheels came off. Lee's only loss had been a 2–1 squeaker to Clanton. The wins were over Tuscaloosa, Holtville, Opelika, Phenix City, and Selma. Then Phenix City paid the Generals back with a 4–1 loss, Clanton won another close one, 5–4, and Lee beat Holtville for the second time, 6–3. Lee was still a respectable 6–4 until a season-ending series with the Lanier Poets. Some more of Coach Chafin's hair came out after Lanier won both games to leave Lee with a 6–6 record, the only year in his career that he did not have a winning season.

Catcher Freddie Johnston, a fullback on the football team, controlled the movement of the infield: Ronnie Beaird at third base, Sim Byrd at shortstop, Wayne Conner at second base, and Billy Bonnett at first. Patrolling the outfield were Lance Wells, Randy Robinson, and Jimmy Kwater. The pitching staff was made up of David Smith, Bill Hust, Jim Tuley, Wayne Mitchell, and Harry Vaughn.

Valuable experience was gained by the juniors and sophomores on the '62 team that would prove to be invaluable in the next two years.

TRACK

Wade Currington, a member of the football and basketball teams, proved to be probably the best athlete at Lee High School. His versatility enabled Lee to score a lot of points in the Alabama State High School Track Meet. He was a member of the championship 440-relay team in 1961. This year he was a member of the 440-relay again in addition to running the anchor leg of the mile relay. And he became the record holder in winning the 440-yard dash in the state meet.

Coach Pete Lee's '62 track team was well represented in the local meets and in the state meet. Running the 440-relay with Currington were Doug Smith, Johnny Tatum, and David Zorich. In the mile relay, Zorich dropped

1962 State Champion Golf Team: from left, Bubba Boone, Rick Rogers, Mac McLendon, Rock Wienard, Carl Alred, Ed Brown Jr., and Ricky Young.

off and Earl Campbell ran the third leg. In the hurdles, Steve Johnson, John Jordan, and Zorich were steady scorers. In the distance races, J. C. Borders, Don Clary, Andy Alpine, Tommy Gowan, and Doug Smith were the iron men. In the field events, Wayne Nobles, Cecil Foster, and David Creel handled the heavy metal. Pole vaulter Phil Hodges had worked hard for two years and was Lee's point getter in that event.

Golf

Lee fielded a golf team for the first time. Coach Pat Garner, having played on the Troy State College golf team, was the best person to pick for the coach of Lee's first golf team. It was obviously a good year to start a golf team. The squad just outplayed every team they played. Then they went to the state tournament and won the Alabama High School state championship.

Mac McLendon was the bell cow of this team. His play, along with that of Ed Brown Jr., Bubba Boone, Rick Rogers, Rock Wienard, Carl Alred, and Ricky Young gave Lee another state championship for the ever-bulging trophy case.

1962–63

Football

The undefeated and untied 1962 Generals were again named AAA state champions. This was the fourth time in five years that Coach Tom Jones's football team won the championship, unprecedented at the time. The Generals were hardly tested by Woodlawn, Tallassee, and Anniston before having a close win over Etowah County, 10–7. The Generals then plowed through Selma, Tuscaloosa, Banks, and Shades Valley. Then Ramsey and Lanier made Lee work for that championship. Ramsey went down 14–7 and Lanier was beaten 7–0 for a season record of 10–0. The state championship came back to Ann Street.

Dickie Waites was the quarterback and captain. Guard Pete Poole and halfback Johnny Beasley served as co-captains. These three seniors provided the leadership of the senior-laden championship team. Beasley was the leading rusher and earned a football scholarship to Mississippi State University.

Senior fullback Walter Warren was like a bulldozer between the tackles. Senior halfback Jimmy Kwater complemented the running of Waites, Beasley, and Warren. Senior fullback Earl Campbell and junior fullback Freddie Johnston provided relief for "Big Walter."

Other seniors who led the Generals to the championship were guards Billy Harper, Gaddis Mann, Phillip Baker, Larry Rhone, Gary Yeck, and Toby Metts. Senior tackles were David Creel, Jay Hopkins, and Glenn Capps. Senior center Ronnie Milligan was the mainstay of the offensive line. Senior ends who contributed were Don Barnhill, Jimmy Mallory, Glenn Shine, and Rex Burleson.

Providing excellent depth for the seniors was an outstanding junior class including quarterback Sim Byrd, tackle Tony Donaldson, guard Ben Joe Cumbus and the Beaird twins, Donnie and Ronnie.

Lee High School football would be left in good hands for the next few years. However, it would be hard to beat four state championships in five years.

BASKETBALL

Coach Leon Ford had left for a college coaching job and was succeeded by Coach Bernard Boyd, a Montgomery native who had been a basketball star at Lanier and then at Troy State College. Although new to Lee, he was an experienced basketball coach. In addition, Coach Pat Garner had been hired in 1961 to coach the "B" football and basketball teams. Garner was the first Lee coach who had played for Lee, having been an outstanding end on the Generals' first football team in 1955. Having had the experience of the previous year, Coach Garner helped make a smooth transition from Coach Ford to Coach Boyd.

Boyd's Generals compiled a 19–7 record, losing twice to Lanier during the season and once in a tournament, and once to Selma in the season and again in the district tournament. Otherwise, the Generals' only losses were to Tuscaloosa and Winfield.

Guards Rusty Keldorph, James Deen, Tommy Gowan, and Sim Byrd made up a strong backcourt. Forwards Rex Burleson, Billy Wilson, and John Enslen provided help from the wings and on the boards. Centers Jim Kranzusch and Ricky Myrick controlled the backboards and the scoring from inside the paint.

WEIGHTLIFTING

Since 1959, Mr. Jerry Windsor had been working with Lee students who were interested in weightlifting. Finally "Coach" Windsor, a teacher on the Lee faculty, got the group that he had been looking for. This team worked hard and used natural talent to win the 1962 state weightlifting tournament. The popularity of the sport had been growing statewide. It was no longer just a club team program, but was recognized by the Alabama High School Athletic Association.

Members of the Lee state championship team were Dickie Waites, Freddie Johnson, Larry Rhone, Ronnie Milligan, Derrell Green, Jimmy Dillard, Tony Clark, Richard Allen, and Randy Stout.

BASEBALL

The 1963 General baseball team again recorded a winning season, Coach

Jim Chafin's eighth straight. Lee won a three game series with Lanier to end the season. Lanier won the first game, 7–3. Then the Generals tightened up the infield and got great work from the pitching staff led by lefthander Wayne Mitchell to squeeze out 1–0 and 2–1 victories. Those last two victories gave Lee a 7–6 record for the year. The losses came at the hands of Phenix City, Opelika, Selma, Troy twice, Phenix City, Tuscaloosa, and Lanier.

Freddie Johnson, in his second year as catcher, kept the Lee infielders on their toes. Third baseman LaBaron Cooper, shortstop Sim Byrd, second baseman Donnie Beaird, and first baseman Billy Bonnett rounded out an excellent infield. Patrolling the outfield were Lance Wells, Tim Dillard, and Jimmy Kwater. The pitching staff was made up of Wayne Mitchell, Johnny Cawthorne, Bill Hust, Harry Vaughn, David Thurman, Greg Tatum, Ben Thornton, and Floyd Maddox.

Track

Coach Pete Lee rolled out his 1963 track team with a squad that was deep in every event, although a lack of the team speed which had characterized past Lee teams hurt in the sprints and the relays. However, Lee got good scoring from the field events. Broad jumpers Mike Mason, Joe Bass, and Eugene Tatum scored. High jumpers Milton Grubbs, Jimmy Gunn, and Albert Marvin scored. Pole vaulters Mike Mason, Albert Marvin, and Joe Gunn scored. Weight men Brad Peek, Mike Morgan, and Ricky Young scored. Points were made in the hurdles with Mike Mason, Steve Johnson, Billy Farrell, and Bob Buls. The mile-relay team of Earl Campbell, Johnny Tatum, David Fletcher, and Billy Hamilton scored well. The distance runners were well represented by Paul Hall, Andy Aplin, Johnny Hall, Robert McFarland, and Mike Bryan.

In the 220-yard dash, Stafford Bice, Jim Tuley, and John Hudson made points. In the 440-yard relay, Danny Glover and John Hudson started it off. Then Johnny Tatum and Stafford Bice brought the baton home. Coach Lee's goal was always to win the state meet. This team came up a little short but provided Lee track fans with many thrills along the way.

Sim Byrd keeps against the Vigor Wolves in the fall of 1963.

Golf

Coach Pat Garner's second edition of the Lee golf team looked a lot like the first one. Players were Tommy Parrish, Mac McLendon, Rock Weinard, Mac Walker, Larry Mayo, Ed Brown Jr., Carl Alred, Doug Crew, and Bubba Boone. This team went undefeated in team matches. The four-man state tournament team of Alred, McLendon, Weinard, and Brown won Lee's second straight Alabama High School Championship. The individual state champion was Weinard. It was rumored that Coach Garner had ordered several sleeves of new balls for next year.

1963–64

Football

Lee in 1963 was on top of the football world among Alabama white high schools. The big schools had been classified for years as AAA. In 1963 the classifications were expanded to 4-A, 3-A, 2-A and 1-A. This didn't bother Tom Jones's Generals. All they did was win the first 4-A Alabama high school state championship. Coach Jones had won five state championships out of the last six years and he and Robert E. Lee High School were becoming nationally known. This '63 team was so good that a 15–7 loss to Tuscaloosa and a season-ending scoreless tie with Lanier could not keep the Generals out of the top spot. Lee beat Ramsey, Vigor, Tallassee, Anniston, Etowah County, Bessemer, Phenix City, and Shades Valley on the way to an 8–1–1 record and the championship.

Captain Ben Joe Cumbus and co-captains Freddie Johnson and Sim Byrd made great senior leaders. Byrd's pinpoint passing won him a football scholarship to the University of Georgia but when Coach Billy Atkins took over the football program at Troy, he was looking for a pro-type passer and punter. He had retired from the Buffalo Bills and was starting his coaching career. He knew that Georgia's Coach Vince Dooley did not throw the football much, so he enticed Byrd to come to Troy. Byrd later led Atkins's Trojans to the NAIA National Championship.

Byrd had plenty of help during Lee's '63 season. Fullback Johnson, halfbacks Johnny Tatum, Larry Meads, Billy Bonnett, Lance Wells, and LaBaron Cooper were called on a lot. Cumbus became one of Lee's greatest guards. Guards Ronnie Beaird, Danny Barber, and Ken Wood were counted on heavily. Seniors Tony Donaldson, Tom Sherman, Warren Marshall, Don Sessions, Dalton Brock, and Mike Morgan were the tackles. Center Donnie Beaird anchored the offensive line with help from Johnny Rowell and Guerry Pruett. Ends Jim Tulley, Joel Stevenson, Tim Dillard, and Billy Hamilton pulled in a lot of Byrd's passes. They were also tough on defense. Other seniors who made great contributions were quarterback Otis Reeves, halfback Delmus Mears, and end Larry Huffstetter.

BASKETBALL

Coach Bernard Boyd's second basketball team had a tough schedule and got off to a slow start, losing four out of the first five games. They opened with a win over Tuscaloosa County. Then they lost four straight to Murphy, Davidson, Enterprise and nemesis Lanier. A win over Alex City was followed by a rematch loss to Tuscaloosa County. A win over Tallassee was followed by a loss to Eufaula. Then came a long winning streak over Kingston, Lanier, Selma, Alex City, Winfield, Tuscaloosa, Tallassee, and Phenix City. Lee won the Montgomery Invitational with wins over Coffee, Dothan, and Lanier. In the Decatur Tournament, Lee beat Union Hill but lost to Decatur 59–57. In the district tournament, Lee won all three games over Central, Dothan, and Lanier, only to lose in the first round of the state tournament to Phillips, 56–55. Lee's final record was 20–10, which included a 3–1 record over Lanier.

Coach Boyd had a great senior class to work with. Forward Tommy Gowan was a three-year starter. John Enslen, Glen Seabury, and Jimmy Harris played well in each game. Junior forward Joel Stevenson showed future prowess. Center Ricky Myrick patrolled the backboards. He was backed up by fellow senior Harry Vaughn. Senior guards Sim Byrd and Jim Tulley helped to control the tempo of the game and force the press on defense.

A talented junior class and some good sophomores awaited Coach Boyd for the next season.

Baseball

Another winning season was achieved by the 1964 Generals with an overall 8–7 record. Three of those losses really should not count, because they were to the Auburn freshman team. Coach Jim Chafin was optimistic with his scheduling in '64. This was one of Coach Chafin's better teams but the schedule was really tough.

Lee lost the first three games of the season to Opelika and twice to the Auburn freshmen. Lee then beat Selma and Troy. They lost the next three games to Lanier, Alex City, and Tuscaloosa for a 2–6 start. Then the talent on this squad started to kick in. Lee won six straight games over Opelika, Troy, Tuscaloosa, Lanier, Alex City, and Selma. The last game of the season was with the Auburn freshmen, a 10–4 loss. The closest the Generals came to beating the Auburn Tigers was in their first encounter in the second game of the season. Lee lost in a close one 5–3.

The Generals were led by a strong senior class. Catchers Jerry Wills and Donnie Beaird were two of the best in the state. Wills's bat drove in a lot of runs. The infield was strong with LaBaron Cooper at third base, Sim Byrd at shortstop, Donnie Beaird or Bill Cleveland at second base, and the ever-steady play of Billy Bonnett at first base. The pitching staff was led by lefthander Wayne Mitchell and righthanders Johnny Cawthorne and Harry Vaughn. Ben Thornton, Floyd Maddox, and Danny Thurman rounded out the pitching staff. Outfielders Lance Wells, Steve Dunn, Ray Engle, and Henry Edwards kept most of the balls in play. They caught most of them on the fly.

TRACK

Coach Pete Lee's last Lee track team was built on depth. Mike Mason and Frank Rudd scored well in the pole vault. In the broad jump, Mason joined Howard Bozeman, Bobby Sims, and Joe Bass. The discus and shot put were handled by Terry DePasquale, Glenn Tatum, and Ricky Young. Steve Johnson excelled in the hurdles. In the distance races, Chip Armstrong, Arlon Poole, Frank Autrey, Paul Hall, and Cliff Cox stretched their stamina for the team. Gary Milton and Stafford Bice ran the 220-yard dash. Other sprinters were Bobby Enslen, David Welch, Elbert Bell, Danny Clower, and John Hudson. In the high jump, Milton Grubbs continued to push for the state championship. Other jumpers were Eddie Nagel, Ken McNeil, Darrel Skipper, and Russ Fox. In the relays, Johnny Tatum and Billy Hamilton led the way with help from David Fletcher, Paul Hall, Clower, and Enslen.

GOLF

Coach Pat Garner put his third Robert E. Lee golf team on the right course. They won their third straight Alabama State Golf Championship, even without the presence of Mac McLendon, who had gone on to star on scholarship at LSU.

The championship team of Larry Mayo, Carl Alred, Ed Brown Jr., and Bubba Boone swept the field for the third straight year. The individual state champion, Brown, had started for three years. The entire squad contributed to the success of this year's team. In addition to the starters, Robert Nation, Butch Bach, and Joel Stevenson were valuable players.

Coach Garner's run of three state championships would come to an end with the 1964 team. He would leave Lee at the end of the school year for another coaching job.

In the 1964 contest against Tallassee, Louis Priester just can't escape!

1964–65

Football

By the fall of 1964 Coach Pat Garner had left Lee for another coaching job. Coach Tommy Hollingshead was hired to be head track coach and coach of the "B" football and basketball teams. Coach Jim Chafin, who had been with Lee from the beginning, and Coach Pete Lee, also a Generaals' veteran, gave continuity to Head Coach Tom Jones's staff.

The Generals made another good run at the state championship, starting 5–0 with wins over West End, Tallassee, Walton, Etowah County, and Bessemer. Then came a tough loss to Tuscaloosa, 16–7. Lee beat Ramsey 16–7, but the next game closed the door on the championship as Dothan beat Lee 32–7, one of the Generals' worst losses to date. Lee got a scare from Vigor, but prevailed 27–26. Then all that was left was to end the year a good note with a 13–7 win over Lanier. The Generals finished the season 8–2.

Captain Joel Stevenson was one of the best ends in Lee football history.

His senior performance earned him a football scholarship to Georgia Tech. Co-captain Ken Wood was outstanding at offensive guard and linebacker, earning a scholarship to the University of Kentucky. Co-captain Jerry Wills was outstanding at tackle even though his real future was in baseball. Wood, Wills, senior guard Mitchell Marshall, and senior tackle Greg Tatum and senior center Terry DePasquale made up one of Lee's best offensive lines. Senior tackles Keith Brewer and Alton James gave Lee outstanding depth in the line. Junior linemen Randy Parker and Buddy Beshears also played a role in the success on the offensive line.

Senior quarterback Bobby Enslen was a tough leader on the field. More a runner than a passer, Enslen impressed Troy Coach Billy Atkins who recruited him as a wide receiver to catch passes from his predecessor Sim Byrd in the NAIA national championship game in 1966. James Turnipseed, Jimmy Middleton, Keith Lampkin, and Wade Johnson added valuable depth to the line.

Senior halfback Louis Priester carried much of the offensive load. He would later play halfback for the Auburn Tigers. Senior halfback Elbert Bell made a lot of great runs. Junior halfbacks Howard Bozeman and Connie Frederick provided depth in the backfield. Frederick would later become a wide receiver and punter for Auburn. Other backs who contributed were Gary Milton, Larry Kwater, Larry Haigler, and Joe Curtis.

Coach Tom Jones had by then finished ten years at Robert E. Lee High School. Five state championship trophies—'58, '59, '60, '62 and '63—for that decade are displayed in the trophy case. During this span Coach Jones had three 10–0 seasons. His record stood at 85–13–2, with four of those losses occurring in his first year. There may never be another ten-year period of success in Alabama high school football to equal this feat.

Basketball

The third time around for Coach Bernard Boyd would not be a good one. For the first time in Lee basketball history, Lee would not end the season with a winning record. This team leaned heavily on the junior class, which bode well for the following year, but it was tough on this team which finished 12–13.

Senior guards Bobby Enslen and Louis Priester were supported by juniors Ray Engle, Connie Frederick, and Steve Dunn. Combined, they made an excellent backcourt team. A considerable lack of height plagued Coach Boyd's squad all season. Junior centers Gary Newton and Harry Ingram were just not tall enough to help on rebounds and short goals. Junior forwards Sammy Johnson and Wayne Evans could not jump with the big guys on the schedule. Therefore Coach Boyd had to experiment with four and five guards on the floor. This worked well as far as scoring but made it difficult under the basket. Senior guard Eddie Smithwick contributed as did senior forward Floyd Maddox.

Baseball

In his tenth year of heading the baseball program, Coach Jim Chafin had to suffer through only his second team to have a losing record. However, the 1965 team did finally beat the Auburn freshmen, 9–8 in the second game of the season. Two one-run losses at the end of the season, 3–2 to Opelika and 6–5 to Lanier cost the Generals that winning record. The baseball team was good. Just a run or two in three games would have turned the season into an 8–4 record. It was not to be.

Catcher Jerry Wills had the big and bad bat. He also directed a good infield led by shortstop Joel Priester and first baseman Steve Dunn. Other infielders were Tommy Traylor, Morris Kellum, Danny Brown, Dory Priester, Buster Neel, Kenneth Bishop, and catcher Keith Green. Coach Chafin had many choices for the outfield. Ralph Hamn, Henry Edwards, Buddy McClinton, and Spence McCracken were available.

This was Coach Chafin's tenth year as coach of the Lee baseball team. In addition to his excellent work as the defensive and line coach of the football team, he had done a marvelous job with the baseball program. A half-century later, he is still one of the most admired and beloved of all Lee coaches.

Track

Coach Pete Lee's team was made up of some excellent athletes in the field events. He also had a group of sprinters and hurdlers who had a chance to be great. They placed in the state meet but could not score enough points to seriously challenge the leaders. This team won several events with other teams in the state before going to the state meet. This team was probably a year away from being a real contender.

Milton Grubbs was the best high jumper in the state. Chuck Cone and Eddie Nagel added depth to the event. George Mills led the weight men along with Glenn Tatum and Mike Kinard. In the pole vault, Frank Rudd was back from last year. He teamed with Mike Teague to give Lee points in that event. The distance races were run by Randy Alford and John Smith. In the mile relay, Gene Melton, Don Garnto, Randy Alford, and John Hudson produced points on a regular basis. In the 440-yard relay, Gene Melton, John Hudson, Davey Welch, and Jimmy Andrews were developing into a good team.

Coach Lee had been building an excellent track program for years. This 1965 squad was one of his first to not include athletes from the football team and the basketball team. That was one of the reasons that this team did not reach the level of a state championship contender.

Golf

Coach Tommy Hollingshead replaced Coach Pat Garner as coach of the Robert E. Lee golf team. This team was missing one top-tier golfer to challenge for the state championship that Lee had owned for three years. Larry Mayo and Ed Brown Jr. were part of the last championship team. Other golfers were Bubba Boone, Tommy Boone, Weldon Doe, Larry Blackman, and James Overstreet.

The 1965 team won most of their individual matches. Brown, who had won the individual championship trophy in 1964, could not get his putter clicking at the state tournament to defend his championship. Sometimes the hole can be smaller than the ball. So it was in 1965.

Generals Pass a Landmark

Although there were marked successes in sports other than football, the first decade saw Lee High athletics known primarily as a football powerhouse. Its meteoric rise to the top of the heap propelled other sports to excel and ignited students, parents, and the entire community of supporters. In the

November 20, 1964, *Stars and Bars*, an article summed up the meaning of football for the school:

> The final whistle at the Lee-Lanier game meant many things besides the end of just another football game. For us Generals it had special significance. It was a major landmark in the history of Robert E. Lee High School. For one thing we had just finished our tenth football season—our hundreth game. Our record for these one hundred games is 85 wins, 11 loses, and 4 ties. This record reveals a much more important truth, though. No school, even the size of Lee, can turn out the material for a winning team ten seasons in a row. The factor that has enabled Lee to realize such an excellent record is an abundance of school spirit—spirit that fills the halls the day of a game, spirit that sends a tingle up and down the spine at a pep rally, and most important, spirit that urges a team on in a crucial point in a game. The fact that Lee has never had a losing season, that we have never been held scoreless in a defeat, and that only two teams in the state have defeated us more than once are all manifestations of this spirit. Lee's first ten years will be forever a pattern for greatness in the state of Alabama.

Roger Stifflemire, president of the "L" club when he played halfback for Lee, fondly recalls that on the bus back from Cramton Bowl after a victory, Coach Chafin always jumped to his feet to lead the team in singing "You Are My Sunshine." He and the other authors of this book harbor the same hope for the future—that the sun should always shine on Robert E. Lee High School.

Roger Stifflemire

9

The Quality of Education

*As Reflected Later in the Lives of Two Dozen
Hall of Fame Members from the First Decade*

"*Fame is no sure test of merit, but only a probability
of such . . .*"

— Thomas Carlyle

By Jim Vickrey

Some 380.
    That is about how many Lee High School graduates, faculty and staff, and others have been inducted into the Lee Hall of Fame from 1994 through 2014. About 240 or 63 percent are Lee graduates (out of approximately 25,000 alumnae and alumni; there is no "official" Montgomery Public Schools figure). Of the 240 alums, some 90, or about 38 percent, are members of one of the first ten classes graduated during the founding decade that is the focus of this book, with the Class of 1960 having the most HOF members.

    The members are memorialized on the Wall of Fame along the main hallway of the school outside the library across from the office. There you'll find an engraved plaque for each Hall of Fame member and each recipient of other awards presented on the occasion of the annual banquet, held each spring in the no longer nostalgically warm school cafeteria.

    The idea for the Lee HOF arose in 1993 in the mind of PTA President Mary Thompson (mother of three Lee graduates). She had noticed a similar effort at Sidney Lanier High School and consulted with then-Lee Principal

James Bozeman (HOF '00). They then asked retired Army Reserve General Russell Berry, the popular former Lee history teacher, to chair an effort to bring about a Lee Hall of Fame. Although Berry was then working for the State, he agreed, but not long afterward he was diagnosed with cancer.

So, Mr. Bozeman, a friend of 40 years, and Mr. Berry, one of my all-time favorite teachers, invited me to lunch in the "Principal's Dining Room" to ask me to co-chair the Lee HOF Committee, deferring to Berry when he was well and assuming active leadership when he was not. I accepted, knowing that they were asking me to chair the inaugural effort as Berry's health deteriorated; indeed, he died not long after.

The original members of the first committee were General Berry and I, co-chairmen, Dr. Louis (Chip) Armstrong, Joanna Crane, LaFreeda Jordan, Jimmy Melton, George Thompson, Mary Thompson (no relation to George), and Barbara Wiggins. From an informal group meeting in the fall of 1993 has evolved a permanent but slowly changing committee of up to 18 elected HOF members. The committee meets three to four times a year, with official minutes and by-laws to memorialize the various procedures and requirements adopted over the years. Mary Thompson and banker Jimmy Melton are the longest-serving members.

"Jimmy" Vickrey ('60), longtime member of the HOF committee, presided over the student council and, in his senior year, weekly assemblies.

Over time, the HOF process became a significant fundraising opportunity for the school (more than $100,000 raised to date), but its major purpose remains what it has always been—to showcase members of the Lee family who have distinguished themselves by their achievements and/or contributions.

The annual calendar of nominations has remained much as it was in the beginning: The cycle starts each year in the early fall with orientation meetings and letters soliciting names; the creating of informational packets for HOF committee members; and determining the date in the spring of the following year on which the next banquet and induction ceremony will take place. The committee then begins to meet in early January to vote on new members, notify them, secure updated information, execute plans, order statues and plaques, and more.

Each HOF inductee gets a handsome reproduction of the statue of Robert E. Lee in the front of the school, a plaque on the Wall of Fame, and a citation—at least one honoree, former biology teacher Marian Marlar, has been buried with the statuette in her coffin.

From the beginning, the committees have sought to honor three categories of Lee-connected persons: successful Lee graduates; former faculty and staff; and persons who have made special contributions to the school by the example of their lives or by significant gifts. Two special awards are also presented at the annual induction banquets: the Becky Sullivan Starr "Spirit of Life" Award (Becky, a cheerleader, was a popular member of the Class of 1960), presented to alums who made extraordinary sacrifice in the course of their lives and/or who dealt heroically with a special challenge; and the General's Award, presented to non-alums who have gone beyond the call of duty as supporters of the school.

That brief background of the Lee High School Hall of Fame understates the many contributions it has made to Lee faculty, staff, and students—from $100,000-plus in gifts to a score of special programs for seniors, featuring successful Lee alums, to generating positive Lee news. The following is a selection of two dozen inductees drawn from the school's first decade—examples of how the Lee education and experience shaped graduates for success in life. They include high achievers from virtually every major profession and walk of life, about whom career information was known beyond the year of their HOF inductions.

Medicine

Dr. Claudia R. Atkison ('60) of Atlanta recently retired from Emory University and from many of her campus and community, not to mention professional, service activities. She studied biological sciences at Huntingdon College, the University of Florida, and later as a graduate student at Tulane University College of Medicine, whence came her Ph.D. degree. The former editor of the *Stars and Bars* rose in Emory's College of Medicine to the level of full professor despite personal tragedy in her private life, before she took time off to pursue a law degree. Thereafter, she practiced intellectual property law with a leading Atlanta firm before returning to Emory as a senior counsel, executive assistant, and legal advisor to the Dean of the Medical School, a position she held until she retired once more to pursue a third career as a medical-legal consultant advising professional clients in medical administration and education around the world.

Dr. Charles Goodwin ('60), a protégé of John M. Long, led the Southernaires Dance Band while a Lee student. After medical school at Tulane University, residencies in Chicago and Kansas City, and a stint as a major in the U.S. Air Force, he became affiliated with the Children's Medical Center in Dayton, Ohio, from 1977 until his retirement a few years ago. He practiced surgical pediatric medicine and taught, researched, served as director of Surgical Education and the Burn Unit, co-directed the Trauma Team, chaired the Department of Surgery, and served as Chief of Staff. Charles regularly won local, regional, and national recognition as one of the nation's leading pediatric surgeons, taught from time to time at the Wright State University School of Medicine, and was published in prestigious medical journals. Last year, he and his wife were named recipients of the Community Founders Award in Dayton. He continues to serve as an advisor to a troop of the Boy Scouts of America and over three decades of leadership has mentored some 229 Eagle Scouts.

DR. BONNIE BRICE DORWART ('60) did her undergraduate work at Bryn Mawr College and then earned her M.D. at Temple University School of Medicine. She has succeeded famously in the fields of clinical and internal medicine, specializing in rheumatology. She deserves special notice for doing her first still-famous major medical research while still in high school; it resulted in every willing Lee High School male student's giving her a urine sample in one of those "precious" little specimen bottles, generating quite an uproar but with it grudging respect for having the moxie to undertake such a scientific project among her male peers.

Other high achievers in the medical and related fields include **DR. ALEX M. JOHNSON** ('62), the Jimmy Hitchcock Award winner who played football under Bobby Bowden at Samford, earned his M.D. at UAB in 1969, returned to Montgomery after a residency and a stint in the USAF, and became the gynecology physician on the staff of Jackson Hospital, where he also served on the board, and in 1989 was named the YMCA Volunteer of the Year; and **DR. DONALD ALAN MARSHALL** ('65), who earned a zoology degree at Auburn before getting his M.D. from the University of Alabama School of Medicine, served a residency in South Carolina and four years in the USAF, returned to Montgomery to set up a family practice, and has served at Jackson Hospital as a staff physician, chairman of the departments of Internal Medicine and Family Medicine, Chief of Staff, and member of the board (caring for the elderly now makes up a large part of his successful practice).

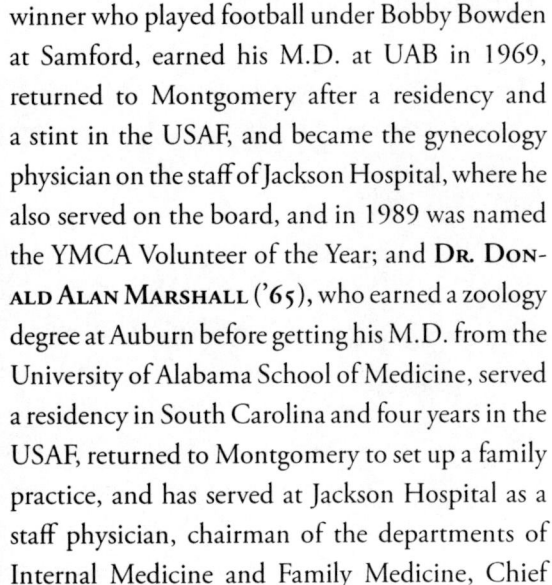

Athletics

BILL MCNAIR ('56) was a three-sport letterman who attended the University of Idaho on scholarship then transferred to and became an all-conference tight end and baseball player at Livingston University. He began his coaching career at Birmingham's Woodlawn High School, where he was Coach of the Year for three of the four years between 1966 and 1969 when his basketball teams won regional championships. Eventually, his resume included eight state championship teams and two awards as National Coach of the Year. While coaching at Thomasville High School, his program was voted Alabama's Most Outstanding Boy's Sports Program.

JOHN TATUM ('64), a member of two Lee state-championship football teams, earned degrees from Troy State and Georgia State universities, and retired after a long teaching and coaching career in Florida, Georgia, and, most recently, at Montgomery Academy, which he joined in 1984 as head football coach and became athletic director in 1995. There he won Coach of the Year Honors in basketball numerous times, a state championship in football, and his teams made postseason appearances in playoff games 13 out of the 18 years he coached at MA. In March 2015, he was inducted into the Alabama Sports Hall of Fame.

DAN WARREN LUCAS ('59) may have the most unusual resume among the HOF athletics honorees. He earned a degree in industrial design from Auburn University and worked at Birmingham's Rust Engineering, but his avocation was in motor sports, particularly drag racing. He competed on the circuits of the National Hot Rod (NHRA), United Drag Racing (UDRA), International Hot Rod (IHRA), and American Hot Rod (AHRA) associations throughout the country. He finished in the top 10 at the division level from 1990 to about

2010 and was clocked at speeds up to 239 mph. He won many honors, including the UDRA Sportsman of the Year Award in 1994. Over the years, he has used his race cars for charity events and taken time to give talks to young people about safe driving.

BUSINESS

CHARLES SIM BYRD ('64) quarterbacked two Lee State Championship teams and went to the University of Georgia on scholarship before transferring to Troy State University where he led the Trojans to the 1968 NAIA National Championship, earning All-American honors and leading the nation in passing. As a result, he is in five halls of fame at the national, state, and regional levels, even though he did not pursue professional sports or coaching and in fact made his post-collegiate success in business. He worked for three Montgomery beverage companies and became president of the Central States Operations for Republic National Distributing Company.

In business, no grouping of HOF members has likely contributed more to the Montgomery community than the brothers KYSER—KYLE ('57) AND JERRY ('59). During careers lasting at least a combined 90 years, involving dozens of separate activities, businesses, and enterprises—and involvement in and support of dozens of River Region civic projects—they have made Montgomery a better place in which to live and work. Their initiatives include the revitalization of downtown Montgomery, including the AlleyWay, and the development of the airport into a regional hub. Since his time as a student at Auburn University, Jerry has been a builder of things—shopping centers, office buildings, apartment complexes, and private

Kyle Kyser

Jerry Kyser

homes—serving as president of the Home Builders Association of Alabama. His greatest impact, however, has been his extraordinary commitment to community service: he has served as chairman of the Montgomery Chamber of Commerce, a member of the Committee of 100, and chairman of the Riverfront Development Committee; he has served on numerous bank and civic boards; and he has built and is still running two of Montgomery's finest restaurants, Central downtown and Garrett's in east Montgomery. Name an activity in the Capital City and Jerry probably has some connection to it or owns the affected real estate or has helped to make it possible—often in joint venture with his brother.

Kyle, also an Auburn graduate, has enjoyed a long and successful career in the retail furniture business and real estate development in central Alabama. His commitment to public service has also been extensive, including chairing the boards or being president of the United Way and the Lions Club, as well as the Blue-Gray Association, Salvation Army, Landmarks Foundation, St. Margaret's Hospital Foundation, Jackson Hospital, and the Red Cross. Moreover, he has been active in and has served as a deacon of Trinity Presbyterian Church.

RAY MCDEVITT ('62) has achieved unusual success in business and science. He was graduated from Auburn University with honors in electrical engineering and began his career at the Harris Corporation, where his first assignment resulted in his first patent and recognition for his inventions. Later, he achieved success and more patents in the then-new field of fiber optics, moving eventually to California's Silicon Valley, where he founded DIVA, a video-on-demand company, and earned his third patent. Thereafter, he joined Microsoft and achieved success there, too, working in particular on Internet Protocol Television systems.

KAY KENNEDY MILLER ('60) was vice president of her senior class and was voted "Most Likely to Succeed," and she has not disappointed. Kay attended Huntingdon College, graduating with highest honor in 1964 and later serving as president of the National Alumni Association. After graduation, she jointed First National Bank, later Regions Bank, and steadily advanced within its ranks to senior VP and a seat on its board. Eventually, she left banking to pursue personal and community interests and has been just as successful. She has served her fellow citizens on the boards of the State Health Planning and Development Agency and the Commission on Aging (both gubernatorial appointments) and on the Stewardship Committee of her church and the Audit Committee of the Alabama Baptist Convention.

ACCOUNTING

JOHN P. LIVINGS ('58), starting end for the first Lee football team, continued to protect the flanks of things he cared about as he attended Auburn University to qualify for the CPA exam. He became an 18-year partner in one of Montgomery's top accounting firms before becoming a founding member of another successful local firm. Eventually, he branched out into residential home building, which led to his becoming president of Wynlakes Homebuilders Association and head of other similar enterprises. His homes have been featured in local publications and in *Southern Living*. But he remains at heart a CPA.

ALBERT I. TARICA ('59) was student manager of the University of Alabama's "Million Dollar Band" and after graduating with a degree in accounting, enjoyed success with national CPA firms as well as with his own firm. He has served as chairman of the Region IV-Georgia Advisory Council of the US. Small Business Administration and worked with other state and federal governmental agencies, in addition to organizing and serving as a board member of a minority bank in Atlanta.

LAW

JOSEPH BECK ('61) graduated from Emory University and served as SGA president before earning his J.D. from Harvard Law School. Thereafter, he earned a Master's of Urban Law degree with highest honor and began practicing in Atlanta. He is now a partner in one of the South's leading law firms, representing artistic and corporate bodies and others in defense of their intellectual property, thereby making himself the go-to guy for many in the entertainment industry. He has also distinguished himself by providing legal services to minorities and indigent persons as well as by being a leader in civil rights. Presently, he is working on a book about a possible miscarriage of justice in an Alabama race-affected rape trial in 1938.

LARRY MORRIS ('61) has had a stellar legal career after graduating from Auburn University and the University of Alabama School of Law, where he was president of the student body. He began his practice in Alexander City, specializing in trial work. Along the way, he has been president of the Alabama Trial Lawyers Association and a member of the Alabama Legislature, as well as a Sunday School teacher. Among his honors are the presidency of the Alabama State Bar and a variety of other state and national legal designations.

ART, MUSIC, AND ENTERTAINMENT

THOMAS R. BORDEN ('60) is a rare HOF member by virtue of being an alum and a former faculty member. An award-winning member of several of John M. Long's best marching bands, Tom earned a B.A. in music education from the University of Alabama and then became assistant band director at Dothan High School. Thereafter, he succeeded the legendary Long when Long moved to Troy State. Directing Lee bands for the next 15 years put Tom at the forefront of high school band-directing in Alabama, with Lee musicians continuing in their All-State ways, at the very time that desegregation was challenging all faculty and staff to find ways to integrate the school without disruption. He and Principal Clinton Carter worked together in the early 1970s to make the band an instrument of conciliation by toning down gratuitous renditions of "Dixie" and displays of the Confederate flag before they could become major issues. Partly as a result of their efforts and of the good will and good sense of students and faculty otherwise, Lee enjoyed an uneventful season of social change. Remarkably, Tom then returned to college and changed careers, earning a second bachelor's degree, this time in accounting from Auburn University. Thereafter, having become a CPA, he joined the firm of Aldridge Borden, where he remained until retirement.

JANET NOLAN ('60) earned a B.A. from Auburn University and an M.F.A. from Georgia State, moved to New York City, and became a specialist in "found art." She scours vacant lots and busy streets for discarded items—gloves, pieces of plastic, colanders, hub caps, umbrella skeletons—from which she fashions remarkable works of art in her studio just blocks from the site of the World Trade Center. Her commissions include works for major universities and hospitals, and her sculpture and drawings have been exhibited in galleries and museums in New York, Chicago, Atlanta, Boston, Sun Valley, Mobile, Auburn, and Denver. She also teaches students how to create and exhibit for themselves works from found materials. "Nightingale," her now-permanent installation at Harvard, was described by a New York art critic as floating "aloft like a flock of birds turning, dipping, preening." Her work may now be found in such places as the Museum of Modern Art and Saint Peter's Church in NYC, but not yet in her hometown.

JAMES W. HUFHAM ('60) seemingly concealed his artistic sensibilities until he had almost graduated from Auburn University, quietly entering fairs and art shows without telling anyone, even while establishing an enviable record as a student leader in fraternal and student government circles. He then earned another B.S. (in chemistry) from the University of Alabama and then a master's degree from the University of Michigan in nuclear power physics, where he studied on a U.S. Atomic Energy Commission scholarship. As the years went by and he excelled in a career in the field of nuclear power, earning awards and honors while working with the Impell Corporation, TVA, U.S. Atomic Energy Commission, and the Nuclear Regulatory Commission in Atlanta, he began to let show his artistic side. His painting, "Winter Wind," has been purchased by the Montgomery Museum of Fine Arts.

Military

JAMES L. HOBSON ('60) had a three-decade USAF career including service in Vietnam flying specially modified C-130 "black ops" planes with small crews and heading several major national and international commands. He commanded the U.S. Special Operations Wing at Eglin AFB and later the Special Forces unit at Hurlburt AFB. Perhaps his highest USAF award, presented in 1983 after the Grenada invasion, is appropriately titled the "Flight of the Year," in his case for piloting the lead aircraft into a hot military zone to deliver U.S. Rangers assigned to rescue American medical students and others from a hostile government on the small Caribbean island. Accounts of the extraordinary flight have been published in military magazines and newspapers. After his retirement as a two-star USAF general, Jim successfully ran an international freight-hauling airline out of Little Rock, Arkansas, moving equipment and such odd cargo as exotic animals.

JAMES W. WARR ('60) was another retired two-star general but in the U.S. Army Reserve. The two-sport Lee letterman worked his way through the reserve ranks after an active-duty career that began in ROTC at Auburn University, where he was simultaneously a distinguished military graduate and the outstanding civil engineering graduate. He saw service in Viet Nam and later earned the M.B.A. degree from AUM and diplomas from a variety of military schools. He combined a successful three-decade-long career in the Army Reserve with a civilian career of equal length—as a civil engineer, first for the Alabama Water Improvement Commission and then the Alabama Department of Environmental Management, eventually becoming director of the latter and earning a reputation for personal and professional integrity.

SCIENCE

JOHN B. SWITZER ('59) left Auburn University in 1963 with a degree in electrical engineering and was employed by NASA at the George Marshall Space Flight Center in Huntsville. Thereafter, over a long career, he distinguished himself and was often commended for his work on the first Saturn V Rocket, receiving the Apollo II Medallion for his contributions. After 1968, he served as a Rocket Scientist with the U.S. Army Missile Command at Redstone Arsenal and managed the Unmanned Aerial Reconnaissance Vehicle which was under development then, the present incarnation of which makes news under the name of "drones." For his scientific work over the years, John has earned awards from such bodies as the German Air Force for help in deploying the HAWK Missile Defense System and from the Redstone Arsenal itself, which presented him the Commander's Medal for Outstanding Civilian Service.

RELIGION

JAMES M. (MICKEY) CASTLEBERRY ('61) was licensed to preach in his junior year at Lee by his home church, Highland Avenue Baptist, and pastored his first church his senior year. Following graduation from Samford University (B.A., 1966), he earned the Master's of Theology degree from the New Orleans Baptist Theological Seminary. Entering the full-time ministry, he returned to school and earned the Doctorate of Ministry from

Luther Rice Seminary in 1978. He served churches in Pike Road, Wetumpka, and Birmingham, the latter being the third-largest church in Alabama. He returned to Montgomery to serve as pastor of Ridgecrest Baptist Church, where he prospered for nine years until health issues required him to retire, taking part in and leading numerous important community and religious activities and receiving many honors. As he withdrew from the active full-time ministry, he founded "Mickey's Ministries" to help people throughout central Alabama, and gave more and more time to the work of the Lee Hall of Fame Committee until his death.

OTHER NAMES COULD HAVE been included above, to be sure, and reasonable persons may disagree as to who more meaningfully represents a given field or profession. The ones chosen, however, are certainly deserving for the purpose, as all are among the 240 Lee alumnae and alumni now constituting the Hall of Fame. That is the nature of such lists, isn't it? It causes us to think comprehensively and to consider for ourselves what selections we might have made. For most of us, merely being included in our Alma Mater's Hall of Fame is recognition enough.

See Appendix B for the complete list of 1994–2014 HOF inductees who were graduated from Lee High School or members of the faculty and staff in place during its first decade.

10

'Echoes' of a Thousand Voices

Footfalls echo in the memory
Down the passage which we did not take
Towards the door we never opened
Into the rose-garden. My words echo
Thus, in your mind.
— T. S. Eliot, "Burnt Norton," *Collected Poems* (1935)

By Jim Vickrey

Walking toward the six doors constituting the Ann Street entrance of our Alma Mater the evening of May 2, 2014, for the annual LHS Hall of Fame induction banquet, I felt General Robert E. Lee's eyes upon me even more than usual. Though I'd emceed the ceremony exactly 54 years earlier during which his weathered bronze statue

The entry to Lee High, pictured in a rare night photo from 1957.

The familiar main lobby, pictured before the opening of school. Also in the lobby (below), Coaches Tom Jones, Jim Chafin, and Pete Lee with the 1962 football state championship trophy. Trophies for 1958, 1959, and 1960 are in the case behind them.

was installed at the entrance to the school, I didn't expect him to remember me well enough to be staring so impolitely. But I felt his gaze nonetheless until I found myself inside the friendly foyer of the 60-year-old physical plant of the largest public school in Montgomery and one of the largest high schools in Alabama. There, I began to feel a different sensation—as though voices from the past were echoing softly off the marble walls, voices of the 3,500 or more Lee students who, like myself, attended the high school in east Montgomery in its first decade, 1955–65.

The voices set me to reflecting upon the first time I ever walked those still-hallowed halls, in an orientation walk-through for rising freshmen from Capitol Heights Junior High one weekday spring afternoon in 1957. I recall other events over the next three years, but, in particular, during our senior year, calling assemblies to order to announce the Homecoming Court . . . to present a visiting speaker . . . to introduce visitors who—on three occasions in Lee's first five years—presented to Head Football Coach Tom Jones, Principal Tim Carlton, and representatives of the football teams, one of the State Championship trophies. Such gatherings in the gym in those days included Bible readings and/or devotionals and concluded with asking all present to stand and recite in unison the last verse of the familiar 19th Psalm: "Let the words of my mouth, and the meditation of my heart, be acceptable in thy sight, O Lord, my strength and my Redeemer."

Similarly, every square foot of Lee High School reminds me still of particular individuals and specific activities and events that left indelible impressions. Walking by "the Office" that night on the way to the HOF banquet, I recalled spending a portion of the first and last days of my senior year there to make the morning announcements. Strolling past the Office, the blond wood of which still frames it with a friendly glow, especially at night, I remembered the many times students were called there to receive messages from home or to retrieve documents related to college-going: the Senior Class Advisor was Mrs. Mary Akers, who coordinated contacts with colleges and universities for us. I also recalled the assistance we always received from Mrs. Louise Smyth, the sweetest "gruff woman" I'd met up to that point in my life, who ran the office for Principal Carlton.

Walking farther east down the main hallway, I passed on my left the

For a half-century, Lee High School's student council presidents presided over the morning announcements each day. Mike Tuley is doing just that in 1962.

Library, domain of Mrs. Virginia Leverette, and the Hall of Fame Wall of Honorees, including the "General's" and "Sullivan's" award" recipients, whose photos remind us "first decaders" of such important REL boosters—many now deceased—as Louis Armstrong, the popular Morningview Baptist pastor and long-time football team chaplain; Paul Robertson Sr., who photographed everything good that happened at and to Lee High and its people the first few decades; George A. "Gus" Dozier, generous local businessman and school board member; W. Travis Dendy, who helped honor the accomplishments of Lee students and raised money to meet school needs; Ed L. Hardin, the popular but strict pastor at Capitol Heights United Methodist Church; Earl D. James, coach, teacher, community leader, and mayor; Foster Goodwin, who was responsible for the first on-grounds scoreboard at Lee and the provision of other needed resources; Sumter Goodwin, whose company kept the lunchroom equipment in order; and school board member and coach Kyle Renfroe, doubtless one of the most effective junior high school coaches in America, whose players dominated Lee varsity athletics its first ten years and beyond, who served on the Montgomery County Board of Education. Those are but a few examples of the extraordinary persons who impacted the Lee student body. Many of those I just named were also parents of Lee students.

All those echoes reverberated as I walked the familiar halls that evening in 2014. But in fact, no matter when I return to Lee or for whatever purpose, I find myself thinking of the people, places, and programs that so powerfully impacted our lives.

In my time at Lee, if one turned right inside at the front doors, one soon walked not into the future auditorium but into the interior south wall of the school. But if one turned left and walked up the short flight of stairs and headed north on that upper first floor, one passed a number of classrooms/home rooms. For my Lee cohort (1957–60), those rooms were presided over by the likes of Latin teacher Mrs. Eunice Day, biology teacher Mrs. Marian Marlar, and English teachers Mrs. Anne Costen and Mrs. Gladys Nichols. On the second floor above that were teachers as idiosyncratically unforgettable as Miss Lola Lawson, a dedicated geometry and math teacher but whose mannerisms invited mischief, or as inspiring as Mr. Russell Berry, who taught American history in such a lively way, as Mrs. Helen Blackshear and Mrs. Corrie King did with English, bringing Arthur and Ulysses alive through Tennyson, for example: ". . . Come, my friends, / 'Tis not too late to seek a newer world. / . . . To strive, to seek, to find, and not to yield."

But, wait; there's more.

Returning to the central corridor directly ahead from the school's front

The west classroom wing, fronting Ann Street, was home to many of Lee's most beloved teachers.

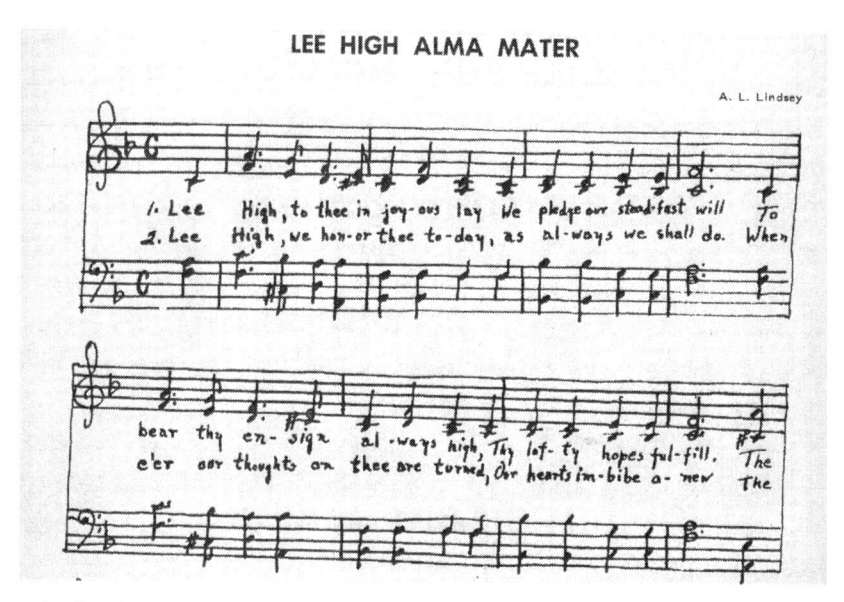

The first bars of the original 1955 manuscript of the Lee High School "Alma Mater," composed by Annie Laurie Lindsey.

doors, about fifty yards ahead a short flight of stairs to the left leads to the back floors of the building to the east.

Walking farther toward the cafeteria, one has to take the short flight of stairs down to ground level and on from there south to the gym or take the aforementioned stairs up to the left. On the upper floors were the likes of Mrs. Addie Adourian, who taught trigonometry and algebra in as clear and straightforward a way as could be imagined and brooked no nonsense but always communicated her confidence in us and our successful futures; Mr. Tom Goolsby, who taught chemistry and made us memorize such as the now unforgettable Avogadro's Number; Coach Pete Lee, who taught English history by outlining the day's lesson in detail on the board and made us copy it word for word in our notebooks (I'm not sure he ever lectured to the class); and Mrs. Marjorie Bagwell, who taught us touch-typing three decades before QWERTY keyboards became ubiquitous in a computerized world. Bless her . . .

Reaching the bottom of the steps just before the doors leading into the cafeteria, I looked to my left and was reminded that at the end of that short hallway was Mrs. Annie Laurie Lindsey's office. She not only wrote the Lee High Alma Mater, which we learned and sang whenever required, she was the student activities advisor and director. In particular, she taught student leaders how to be such and instructed us in the arts such roles required of us. She also had on occasion to put up with our immaturity.

Every first decader's experience would be unique, but I think most of us could agree on some memorable lessons we learned at Lee. As a starting point, I offer these ten, without regard to which teacher, coach, or staff member might have instilled the lesson:

—A person of principle has fewer negative encounters with the Principal;

—Everyone works for someone or some board or some higher authority;

— Each of us has a level of personal competence above which we ought to have little confidence in our work;

—Lying as a matter of routine always fails in the long run;

—Respect those in authority, even when they are wrong, and use established channels of communication to seek to inform their discretion;

—Read widely, including especially nonfiction, and take notes;

—Observe and record pithy, quotable remarks of notable persons;

—Remember, people are usually more important than principles;

—Learn grammar, apply it, and learn how to spell, including other person's names;

—Respect sources as you respect yourself: quote them accurately and use them only with appropriate attribution.

Those of us fortunate to be among the favored first decade of students at Robert E. Lee High School in Alabama's Capital City received a grand start: we got a first-rate high school education from top teachers at a special time in American history, between the "take a breath fifties" and the "breathless sixties." We've traded on it all of our lives.

Let's "pay it forward" for those yet to receive high school educations by insisting that Montgomery today and tomorrow do just as well by present and prospective students as it did by us yesterday.

One way to do that is to ensure that there'll always be a Robert E. Lee High School still building on the tradition of its founding.

Above, an artist's rendering of the original front entrance of Lee High School. Below, Lee's library, pictured here in the fall of 1955, was modern and well equipped for the time period.

11

A New Vision and Beginning

"Education . . . I view as the most important subject which we, as a people, can be engaged in."
— Abraham Lincoln (first public political statement, Illinois, 1932)

By Jim Vickrey

All living individuals as well as institutions have futures; else they would be dead or dying. In looking to the future of Robert E. Lee High School, therefore, it is important that we acknowledge possible outcomes for what has been since its founding sixty years ago one of the great public high schools in the history of this state.

Our Alma Mater on Ann Street exists in the very same public school system that has recently boasted the nation's "number one high school": the Loveless Academic Magnet Program. LAMP's success didn't just happen; the school has achieved its status as a result of the conscious choices made by past and present academic leaders and the positive responses to its rigorous program of thousands of parents and students over the period of a mere quarter-century.

Will the same be said of "the new Lee High School" which has been a part of the facilities-planning in the Montgomery Public School system over the past decade?

Answering that question should first remind those of us who care most about the possible futures of Lee High School that nothing has yet been cast in concrete. It is not already determined whether Lee High School will stay where it is and be renovated, with or without the same name, or will remain where it is in name only as we await its being razed and rebuilt, or

The Lee Auditorium, pictured under construction in 1962, was one of the most modern public performance spaces in the state when it opened in 1964.

will be moved to a new site in northeast Montgomery County with the same or a different name. Those possible outcomes are policy choices that people will make and try to shepherd through the system.

Let us consider three related questions that can help us to answer the first and so participate in shaping the Lee future.

First is the facility issue: What is required by way of financial resources to recover and then to maintain the level of academic and other programmatic, personnel, and physical facility resources our Alma Mater once enjoyed, enabling it to arrive again at the top levels of the secondary school market?

Second: What is the status and priority of the DeJong-led Facilities Report recommending the relocation and reconstruction of a new Lee High School?

Third, and overlapping the other two questions: What must partisans of Lee High School do in the next five to seven years to ensure that funding and politics are joined to enable the "new Lee High School" to come into existence under present reporting documents?

In the near future, decisive action must be taken by the Board of Education to deal with the evolving crisis in the deterioration of the physical facility named Robert E. Lee High School.

First, the physical plant is sixty years old, never having been renovated or improved with major repairs other than re-roofings. Deferred maintenance is as much of a growing problem as in any school in the MPS.

Second, Phase One of the "Ann Street Widening" is underway but will not much affect Lee as it ends just in front of the school. But if and when Phase Two is approved and funded, it will have a major negative impact, for its completion will require the taking of most of the front Ann Street portions of the site, up to near the base of the Lee statue. One reason is that Phase Two dictates angling Ann Street sharply to the right before it gets to the Atlanta Highway to allow a straight connection into Federal/William Dickinson Drive. While Mayor Todd Strange says that neither final plans have been approved nor final funding secured for the whole project, in politics things have a way of changing rapidly.

Thus, third, what is needed to preserve Lee's academic and athletic traditions is solving the physical facility problem, planning proposed sites and structures, properly preparing attendance zones, and beginning to do the things that were contemplated by DeJong and the local facilities committee when they developed priorities, cost estimates, and the like.

Of the three available options—renovation; razing and reconstruction on site; or construction of a new facility at another location in northeastern Montgomery—the consultants and the committee recommended the latter to the Board of Education. Why? Because it was thought to be more cost-effective and convenient for students and faculty and in the interim would be less disruptive to current Lee classes and other important activities.

It is estimated that building a new equivalent to Lee's Ann Street complex would cost around $40 million (exclusive of new personnel, programs, lab equipment, or other incentives to attract and keep the sort of students who increasingly are the difference between excellent and mediocre schools). The investment, however, would be well worth the price and might well lead to the return of families who have left the public school system. And that,

Lee students during the first decade enjoyed one of the cleanest and most modern school plants in the state.

arguably, would change everything for the better in Montgomery County.

What is imperative is that the Board make a decision on Lee High School and then follow through on that commitment. A tactical decision to renovate on-site or a strategic decision to raze and reconstruct it or simply to walk away from the site to be sold as is.

The original 2010 De-Jong Facilities Committee Report stated that (1) the Board should establish a High School Reform and Restructuring Committee and (2) establish two priorities for addressing high schools in the MPS district. Priority 1 was for a new high school on the east side. Priority 2 was that Lanier High School should be renovated to house BTW and LAMP (the arts and academic magnet high school programs, respectively).

Priority 1 has been fulfilled in the form of the new Park Crossing High School. Instead of implementing Priority 2, the Board of Education has recently determined to renovate space in the old Montgomery Mall and move LAMP into it.

A third priority was to replace Robert E. Lee on a new site to be determined.

I was a member of the Facilities Committee, which met publicly many times in a variety of places. I observed that the Lee recommendation originally had a higher priority than in the final report presented to the Board.

That original and still operative report can be compared profitably with the Board's current facility priorities. Carefully comparing the two lists is cause for both pessimism and optimism. The latter because we are nearly completed with some previous priorities, effectively moving "the new Lee High School" up on the lists; the former because there is virtually no additional present funding expected to be coming into the MPS that would permit even a small portion of the nearly $400 million in total identified needs.

The term "the new Lee high school" is not used in the reported recommendations for reasons that are not clear. Throughout the deliberations of the committee over a period of months, that phrase was used on all of the DeJong documents, involving multi-year stages, distributed to us as staff materials to stimulate discussion and debate. The documents accurately captured what the consultants consistently recommended be the fate of Lee High School: a new physical plant built elsewhere, preferably in the northeast quadrant of the city-county, somewhere near the former front entrance of Gunter AFB along what used to be called Federal Drive (now William Dickinson Drive).

The "Capital Plan Layout Report," dated August 6, 2014, but provided to the committee in mid-December 2014 was explained to me in detail by the highly informed, impressively competent, inspiring MPS Assistant Superintendent of Operations Donald Dotson. He pointed out that of the 50 projects listed on the document, "Lee High School" is number 16, with a paper budget of $40 million, a funding year designation of 2018, and "Funding Source Unknown"—the same funding designation noted for all except the first 10 listed. Those first 10 capital projects have already been funded and completed or are on the way to completion. Moreover, five involve "Roofing Only," two are planned "Renovations" of existing facilities, two involve "HVAC" improvements or replacements, and one is "Additions" to an existing facility.

Of the next five projects with a higher priority than "Lee High School," only one involves a "New School," which in reality is merely LAMP's imminent move to Montgomery Mall; the others all involve either "Additions" at Park Crossing, which is being built in phases, "Renovations" at two schools, and "Land Acquisitions." Lee's listing at number 16 is labeled "Building Replacement," the first of the next four such designations rounding out the top 19 projects named.

It can be seen, therefore, that the replacement of Robert E. Lee High School at a new site with a budget of $40 million is the highest priority new facility on the Board's list of 50 projects now totaling some $400 million.

Mr. Dotson, however, told me that several possible sites for a Lee replacement school in northeast Montgomery were examined recently in connection with the Board's finalizing the 50-item report. Lee partisans can be encouraged that the priority for the Lee Project has remained high and that preliminary site selection has been undertaken. Unfortunately, as Dotson kept reminding me during our free-wheeling conversation, none of the money is presently available for new buildings beyond those noted above. Indeed, Montgomery County Board of Education members do not have access to capital funding, other than (1) the Legislature's special appropriations; (2) the selling of bonds related to the purpose of a given facility; and/or (3) private donations.

Public high schools play many roles in school systems, including serving as "capstone institutions." Public school systems rarely rise above the quality level of its best high schools. There is presently at least one high school of demonstrable quality in each of the district zones in Montgomery, with the exception of the northeast quadrant of the county where "the new Lee High School" is to go. Let us pray that funding for it and for other MPS needs is identified in the near future, or, in the case of the "Lee High School" project, by the indicated Funding Year date: 2018.

It will not just happen, however. To some extent, Lee partisans must do what they are already doing—meeting and talking on a regular basis between five-year reunions. Some have been meeting monthly for dinner for most of the past ten years. [See Boland report, Appendix B.]

Lee graduates have also played roles in school board elections, sounding out the views of candidates on such things as moving and rebuilding Lee High School elsewhere. From time to time, a majority of the school board and/or the superintendent have/has indicated clear support to move and rebuild Lee. Turnover on the board and in the superintendent's office has been such over the past five years that maintaining that support at a given level is always a challenge, but one that must be continually met until the job is done and the future of Alma Mater is bright again.

Over the past 22 years, hundreds of Lee alums—some from thousands of miles away—have returned to take part in the annual Hall of Fame banquet and induction ceremony, dine again in the now blessedly air-conditioned facility, catch up on old times and current events, and contribute tens of thousands of dollars to Lee academic programs. As a result, many Lee alumni are well informed about local politics, including the state of educational funding in Alabama, almost always in crisis mode but made more challenging the past 25 or so years because of the overlay of local racial politics. The latter has complicated things and made joint action to generate better funding for public education in our state that much more difficult. Nevertheless, the proverbial die has been cast and now many Lee alumni know what is at stake and what the major options are, making the matter too important to be ignored by the Board of Education.

I hope we can maintain that interest, build upon it, and show once again that "the mode through which the inevitable comes to pass is effort," the concerted efforts of persons who have benefited from exposure to the best of the academic opportunity Lee High School represents, and who see no reason why students coming after us, even long after, should not have the same foundation for a successful personal and professional life.

Obviously, the continuation of a school or the building of a new one named for a pardoned Confederate hero will be an issue in any future decision-making. However, the real battle will almost certainly be over securing adequate funding to meet the school system's continuing need for better facilities, up-to-date equipment for classes and labs, and the like; it should not be permitted to be anything else, particularly an ill-fated, anachronistic verbal war that would divert attentions and misplace the focus of the debate.

In concluding this chapter and this book, I would only add a remark attributed to French essayist Montaigne about public approval of one's voiced opinions: "I speak truth, not so much as I would, but as much as I dare; and I dare a little the more, as I grow older."

Appendix A

A Note of Special Recognition of Mr. Richard Jordan

CLINTON CARTER

Heartfelt thanks go to Mr. Richard Jordan, a 1958 Lee graduate who graciously provided financing for the publication of this book as a tribute to Mr. Tim Carlton, Lee's first principal. Mr. Carlton was pivotal in mentoring and securing financial support for Richard as he made his way through Lee, the University of Alabama Business School and The School of Law, also at the University of Alabama.

For several years, Richard and I discussed an appropriate vehicle to honor Mr. Carlton. Eventually we settled on the idea of funding this publication as the best way to recognize him as the man who guided Lee through its foundational years.

It was my pleasure to initially interview Richard in his law office on September 18, 2014; this was followed by subsequent interviews, phone conversations, and correspondence. I wanted to know not only about his special relationship with Tim Carlton, but also what I soon saw was a man who through great determination overcame obstacles to reach his goals. His story, briefly memorialized below, should be an inspiration to every young man and woman who aspires to succeed.

Richard was born in Elmore County in what is usually referred to as "Beat 14." From there, he moved to the Chisholm area where he resided at 61 Pickett Street with his mother, grandmother and two younger brothers. The Pickett street home, purchased for $1100, remained his home until after his graduation from law school. His father passed away when he was very young and his mother, possessing only a fourth grade education, supported the family by working in a local cotton mill, while struggling all her life with asthma.

Richard recalls that his elementary school years at Chisholm Elementary (1945–51) were routine and uneventful, but he does recall that his teachers were "God sent." He enrolled at Capitol Heights Junior High School in September 1951 where during his three years he earned only mediocre grades and he was unable to gain focus on a future that did not extend beyond finding a job and eventually buying a car, which his family had never owned.

Even at such an early age, Richard was already engaged in a number of jobs, including helping with a paper route and working in a barber shop shining shoes to name only two. It was at Capitol Heights that Richard had his first encounter with Tim Carlton, having first been shaped by the strict discipline of Coach Kyle Renfroe, the first male to have had a positive influence on his life. Mr. Carlton, knowing of Richard's financial stress, offered to get him a job driving one of the school buses at Capitol Heights, predicated on his getting a drivers license. Richard was only 14 at the time, but somehow, perhaps foretelling his future success as an attorney, he was able to secure the license and earn $30 each month for his work. Also, and perhaps foretelling his future success in business, he had business cards with "Richard Jordan, School Bus Driver" printed on them. He graduated from Capitol Heights at the end of the summer session in 1954.

Richard enrolled at Lanier High School in the fall of 1954. He was not a good student and his goal was to remain in school only until his age exceeded the compulsory attendance law and to enter the work force, which was the expectation of the culture at that time. Making good on his goal, he withdrew from Lanier on April 4, 1955 and thereafter worked a number of jobs, including employment during the summer of 1955 with Moss Construction Company installing a pipeline across the Kilby Prison property and working at the service station on Gunter Air Force Base, where on the days he was off he developed a side line waxing cars for officers assigned to the base. It was not long after Richard withdrew from Lanier that the germ of an idea formed that would transform him from an individual adrift to one who was focused on gaining an education and becoming successful in life. He simply determined that no matter what it took he was going to make something of himself beyond working at jobs requiring only a strong body, and it was at this point that Tim Carlton, newly named as Lee's first principal, reentered his life. Richard went to see Mr. Carlton before the beginning of the 1955–56 school year. The Chisholm area had become a part of the Lee attendance zone; thus Richard could not have returned to Lanier. His appeal to Mr. Carlton was met with a frosty response and his plea for enrollment was rejected. The fact that Richard owned a car and owed payments indicated to Mr. Carlton that it was unlikely that Richard would remain enrolled. That, coupled with Richard's poor prior academic performance did not indicate to Mr. Carlton that he would ever complete high school. Richard reapplied for enrollment in January 1956. The issue of the car was settled when Mr. Tommy Duncan, an adult mentor to Richard, informed Mr. Carlton that he would pick up the payments. The issue of the poor academic performance was settled when Richard agreed that if allowed to enroll he would come one hour early each day for tutoring.

With those two issues resolved, Richard became a member of the Lee student body in January 1956. His tutors included some of the most experienced and effective teachers at Lee, including Miss Gladys Nichols, Mr. Russell Berry, Mrs. Marjorie Bagwell, and Mrs. Mary Akers. With a change in attitude, a focus on the future and with the help and encouragement of many Lee teachers, Richard's grades began to improve throughout his high school years. He received his diploma with the third graduating class on May 30, 1958. Now what? Richard had a high school diploma and a desire to become an attorney with an ultimate goal of holding elected office; but, with no money, how could that become a reality? Tuition at the University of Alabama at that time was $87.50 per semester with student activity fees of $12.50, a total of $100 per semester.

Once again, Tim Carlton came to his rescue, convincing the Elks Club to give Richard $200 that would satisfy his tuition and student fees for the first year at the University of Alabama. Richard was accepted on a conditional basis and required to take remedial courses because of his less than sterling academic performance throughout his schooling. That soon changed because of his determination to succeed and his grades began a steady movement upward, continuing through the completion of his BS degree in Commerce and Business Administration and then law school. The icing on the cake, as one would say, is the fact that Richard served as the Law School Student Body President in 1964. Richard's "hustle," as he would call it, enabled him to earn other funds by working at a number of part time jobs in Tuscaloosa, such as the Corner Drug and Malone Bookstore.

His participation in the Senior ROTC four-year program, in which he was later named as one of 25 Distinguished Military Students, also allowed supplemental funds of $30 per month and earned him a commission as a

Second Lieutenant in the Army. A photograph of his mother pinning on his bars was proudly displayed in the newspaper of the cotton mill where she worked. Other than the contribution from the Elks and his part time jobs, including a summer stint in the ticket office of the L&N Railroad in Montgomery, Richard received no additional financial support from the efforts of Mr. Carlton until January 1961. At that point, Mr. Carlton tapped into the Bessie Bartlett Student Loan Fund, started with Richard specifically in mind, loaning him enough money to satisfy his tuition and cost of books which continued until January 1964.

At Mr. Carlton's retirement in June 1970, Richard headed a committee to organize a ceremony recognizing Mr. Carlton's service to Lee High School. In response, Mr. Carlton wrote a letter of thanks to Richard in which he stated "You grew even taller in my eyes by your statements at my testimonial dinner. I appreciate your friendship and your loyalty. You will always be one of my heroes for overcoming the obstacles that you have to become the man that you have become." After earning his law degree, the first Robert E. Lee High graduate to do so, and which Richard describes to have been the most important event in his life, he returned to Montgomery where he established his practice under austere circumstances, but where he soon gained recognition as an energetic and determined attorney and where he has enjoyed a productive and satisfying 50-year career in the legal profession.

Richard's interests are eclectic. He has an on-going curiosity about wide-ranging topics in life. He continues to enjoy his interest in aviation and competitive clay shooting, remaining competitive in that sport both nationally and internationally at the age of 76. Though semi-retired from the practice of law, Richard continues to consult on selected court cases from his office near the Montgomery County Courthouse. He is married and he and his wife, Lee, have one son, Shane Jordan, a daughter Shannon Jordan Abbott, and grandchildren Ben, Luke, Reed and Libby.

Without the assistance of Richard Jordan it is doubtful that this book could have been published. Those who read and enjoy it owe a large debt of gratitude for his support.

Appendix B

1955–65 Graduates, Faculty/Staff, and Others Inducted into the Robert E. Lee High School Hall of Fame

INDUCTED 1994
Claudia R. Atkison ('60)
Bonnie Brice Dorwart ('60)
Faye Barfoot Gaston ('61)
Dalton Guthrie ('57)
Lester Henderson ('58)
James L. Hobson ('60)
James F. Vickrey ('60)
Laura Childree Young ('60)
Faculty
Russell Berry ('55–'66)
Tim Carlton ('55–'70)
Tom Jones ('55–'66, '75–'77)
John M. Long ('55–'65)
Louise Smyth ('55–'71)
Special Award—Rev. Louis Armstrong

INDUCTED 1995
Ben Joe Cumbus ('64)
Charles Goodwin ('60)
Peter Howard ('63)
Sarah Graham Norred ('57)
John Bowman Switzer ('59)
Faculty
Clinton Carter ('62–'70, '70–'80)
James R. Chafin ('55–'72)
Joanna Breedlove Crane ('55–'60)
Gladys Nichols ('55–'75)
General—Foster Goodwin
Spirit of Life—Becky Sullivan Starr

INDUCTED 1996
Joseph Beck ('61)
Thomas Gilliland ('64)
Alex M. Johnson ('62)
Larry Morris ('61)
James W. Warr ('60)
Faculty
Helen Blackshear ('56–'73)
Ellyn Dudley ('55–'74)
Julia Shell ('57–'70, '70–'95)
General—Kyle Renfroe
Spirit of Life—Linda Jemmott Chambliss

INDUCTED 1997
Buddy Davidson ('57)
Bill Harper ('63)
Joseph McGilberry ('61)
Dutchie Riggsby ('59)
Thomas Turner ('64)
Faculty
Fred Guy ('59–'80, '80–'91)
Marian Marlar ('58–'87)
Paton Woodham ('55–'60)
General—Earl James
Spirit of Life—Wayne Mitchell

INDUCTED 1998
David Dillard ('59)
Kay Kennedy Miller ('60)

Michael Tuley ('62)
Faculty
Addie Adourian ('55–'69)
General—Mary Thompson ('69)
Spirit of Life—Renny Mize

Inducted 1999
Ronald Godbold ('61)
Debbie Rice Johnson ('62)
Fred Suggs ('65)
John Tatum ('64)
Faculty
Ledford Boone ('55–'62)
Jennie Cain ('61–'98)
Leon Ford ('55–'62)
General—Don Walker
Spirit of Life—Mary Beth Shouse Dodson

Inducted 2000
James M. Castleberry ('61)
Kyle Kyser ('57)
Paul Ohme ('59)
Joe Wingard ('62)
Faculty
Marjorie Bagwell ('55–'66)
James Bozeman ('62–'94)
Corrie King ('55–'69)
Pete Lee ('57–'75)
General—Kathleen Hale
Spirit of Life—Clinton Rowell

Inducted 2001
Jerry Kyser ('59)
Donald Alan Marshall ('65)
Janet Nolan ('60)
Albert I. Tarica ('59)
Faculty
Josephine Grissette ('55–'70)
General—Frank E. Huey

Inducted 2002
William Bonnett ('64)
Roy Parker ('62)
Ed Reynolds ('65)
Woody Weaver ('61)
Faculty
Eva Carr ('56–'64)
Grover Jacobs ('61–'72)
General—Sam H. Wingard Sr.

Inducted 2003
Sandra Best ('59)
Wade Currington ('62)
Mary Ellen Dendy Harp ('60)
Darrell Skipper ('64)
Faculty
Chris Green ('59–'87)
Sammye Norton Jackson ('57–'92)
General—Billy M. Turner
Spirit of Life—Martha Crystal Meyers

Inducted 2004
Donald Davis ('58)
Jim Spear ('57)
Faculty
Annie Laurie Lindsey ('55–'70)
General—Travis W. Dendy
Spirit Of Life—Eudora Rodgers Godley

Inducted 2005
Mary Ann Pugh Arant ('58)
William Cherry ('64)
Richard Garrett ('65)
Judson Huett ('56)
Durden Lee ('56)
Robert Ritter ('61)
Roger Stifflemire ('60)
Faculty
Dollie Clements ('63–'89)

Anne Costen ('58–'75)
Spirit of Life—Kenneth R. Hammett

INDUCTED 2006
Barbara Boland ('60)
Pat Garner ('56)
James W. Hufham ('60)
John Livings ('58)
Nell McGilberry ('59)
Ted Watts ('65)
   FACULTY
Carol Hyland ('65–'69, '88–'94)
Norma Johnson ('62–'87)
General—George A. "Gus" Dozier

INDUCTED 2007
Frank Autrey ('64)
Otis Reeves ('64)
Donnie Tucker ('59)
   FACULTY
Sam Kennedy ('62–'71)
General—Frank Jackson
General—Glenn Fair Palmer
Spirit of Life—Barbara Kenda Horton

INDUCTED 2008
Chuck Edwards ('61)
Billy Thames ('58)
General—Paul Robertson Sr.
Spirit of Life—Joseph Lancel "Lance" Wells

INDUCTED 2009
George McCain ('62)
Laurens Pierce ('60)
Ann McLean Spear ('64)
Five Star General's Award—Clinton Carter
Spirit of Life—Lena Frances Dean Skipworth

INDUCTED 2010
Ed Jones ('56)
Dan Warren Lucas ('59)
Grant Sullivan ('64)
Jerry Wills ('65)
Spirit of Life—Murray Conrad "Connie" Frederick

INDUCTED 2011
George Beasley ('61)
Ken Groves ('64)
Walter Horn ('63)
Claudia Spence Jack ('61)
Travis Scott ('61)
Fred Woolard ('58)
General—Leroy Pierce
Spirit of Life—Joseph Nelson Jr.

INDUCTED 2012
Charles Sim Byrd ('64)
Charles Milton Deas ('63)
Thomas Gowan ('64)
Marie Little Parma ('56)
Spirit of Life—Jane McSwain Thrash and Ed "Rudy" Thrash

INDUCTED 2013
Robert G. Enslen ('65)
Rhonald Jenkins ('60)
Doug Lindley ('64)
Ray McDevitt ('62)
Bill McNair ('56)
General—Bob and Dianne Brooks

INDUCTED 2014
Louise Smith Blake ('57)
Sara Ann Dubose ('59)
Spirit of Life—Janice Goode Cruce

Appendix C: Alumni Activities

Many of Lee's graduating classes have reunions on a five-year schedule. Some classes hold interim reunions or informal get-togethers on a much more frequent schedule and have developed other ways to keep in touch. Below are two examples.

Class of 1959

In addition to its regular reunions, this class also sometimes meets at Arrowhead Country Club in Montgomery. It also has a subset called the "LaGrange Group." Including up to 50 Lee alums, most of whom also attended Auburn University around the same time, the thus far all-male group first met several years ago in LaGrange, Georgia, hence its name. It now meets for lunch roughly bi-monthly at the Lodge in Callaway Gardens, a half-way point between Atlanta and Montgomery. At the latter meetings, in particular, reports are often made on projects or problems. The same alums and many others also stay in touch via email.

Class of 1960

(An Activity Report by Reunion Chairperson Barbara Boland)

The Robert E. Lee Class of 1960 has remained connected throughout the years since its graduation May 27, 1960. That connectedness has been fostered through various approaches: class reunions, monthly dinners, emails, cards, letters, visits, phone calls, and individual friendships. We have extended our class friendships beyond the close friends we had in high school as have shared in the lives of each other.

Each of us has grown and matured in ways we could not have fathomed when we left the hallowed halls of Lee High School. We had not scratched the surface of our potential. We are constantly tuned into news about our classmates. Sadly to say, we sometimes only find out the accomplishments of our classmates through obituaries. As one of our classmates wrote, "There are so many interesting stories in the Class of '60. Each decision made along the way created a complex life with struggles and blessings." These stories are of classmates who are/were medical professionals, educators, scientists, missionaries, military commanders, artists, business persons and many other meaningful careers.

At our 45th reunion in August 2005, someone announced that we would begin having a monthly class dinner. We began gathering on a monthly basis the following month at different restaurants. After about three months, we settled on Sinclair's on Vaughn Road. We outgrew our space at Sinclair's after about four years and decided to meet at Arrowhead Country Club. We have been meeting at Arrowhead since July 2009 on the fourth Thursday of each month. We have never cancelled a single month. Our connectedness grew out of the experiences of sharing with each other at these dinners. It has been fun and interesting to watch classmates interact with other classmates they had no connection with in high school. This congeniality has fostered a respect and caring spirit that transcends the Montgomery area group. [It has also facilitated information-sharing about and participation in local educational political activity impacting the present and future status of our Alma Mater, enabling us, even on short notice, to turn out Lee advocates at meetings of the County Board of Education.]

In 2005 we began maintaining contact with each other via email. (Such does not leave out classmates who lack email. But, many of those classmates have someone who has email, finding out the news through that person.) When there is joy or sadness in the life of a classmate, we send out the news to everyone. We include contact information for that person or family member. If we have a picture of the person from our 1960 *Scabbard*, we include it in the email. That prods our memory of the classmate. The interest and response to these messages has been amazing. One recipient with terminal cancer attached the numerous cards he received around the door facings in his bedroom. He had a constant reminder of that caring spirit and support that is so prevalent among our classmates. One classmate who lives in North Alabama was treated for multiple myeloma at the Myeloma Institute in Little Rock, Arkansas. Another classmate who lives in Little Rock reached out to offer his support. No matter where we are, we know we are not alone. We have a network of friendships from our class. So many have said what a blessing it has been to receive encouragement through emails, cards, letters, visits and phone calls from our classmates from 1960.

The Robert E. Lee Class of 1960 has shown a commitment to each other that has sustained a closeness for over 50 years. We realize we have gone separate ways and have many new friends, but it is comforting to know we have the long-ago friendships from our youth. That was truly an amazing time with amazing classmates.

Contributors

CLINTON CARTER (HOF '95) is a graduate of Troy University and Auburn University and was a teacher and administrator, Lee's assistant principal (1962–70), principal (1970–80), and assistant and associate superintendent (1981–95) of the Montgomery Public Schools. He was called out of retirement to become the MPS superintendent from 1998 to 2004. He was honored with the unique "[Five Star] General's Award" in 2009.

TOM HAMMETT ('67; HOF '14) was Student Director of the Choralees and an All-State drummer. He earned music education degrees from Troy University and Florida State University. He is a former member of Atlanta Symphony Orchestra Chorus under Maestro Robert Shaw.

ROBIN BOZEMAN HARDWICH ('67; HOF '09) was a Lee cheerleader, class beauty, and senior homecoming attendant. She returned to Lee as a teacher and director of activities, devoting 30 years of her career to the school.

DEBBIE KNIGHT HOOKS ('71; HOF '14) was the head varsity cheerleader, Miss Lee High, and president of the Senior Class. Following high school, she became a teacher and counselor, serving in several public and private schools.

PETER HOWARD ('63; HOF '95) is a professor of foreign and classical languages at Troy University. Educated at the University of Alabama and Florida State, he worked for the U.S. Army Security Agency, was chairman of the Troy Department of Foreign Languages, and chief faculty consultant for the national Advanced Placement Latin Program. He was state vice president of the Classical Association of the Middle West and South.

RHETA GRIMSLEY JOHNSON ('71; HOF '95) went from middle and high school student journalism to the editorship of the *Auburn Plainsman* and then on to a distinguished career as a reporter, columnist, and author. She has won many national newspaper awards and was a finalist for the Pulitzer Prize. She is the author of five well-received books and her popular weekly newspaper column is nationally syndicated by King Features.

ED JONES ('56; HOF '10) participated in football, chorus, and was on the staff of the *Stars and Bars*. Following high school he served in the Marine Corps before earning a college degree. He subsequently taught and coached at Lanier and Montgomery Catholic High. He continues to use the skills learned as a member of Lee's newspaper staff in his current work as a sports writer and commentator.

KERRY PALMER ('90; HOF '14) was the drum major at Lee and Troy University. A protégé of Lee Marching Band director and HOF member John M. Long, he is Head of School at Trinity Presbyterian School, Montgomery. He previously headed its Middle School.

WILLIE RIGGINS JR. ('65) was drafted and spent two years in the Army, including being wounded in Vietnam. After returning to Montgomery, he managed several McDonald's stores and a neighborhood grocery. He then worked for the State of Alabama until his retirement in 2010 and remains a Montgomery resident.

JULIA SANDERS ('65) encountered job discrimination after graduating from Lee. She moved to Detroit for a time, where she worked for AAA insurance, then returned and landed a position with the State of Alabama. Retired after 40 years of service, she lives in Montgomery.

ROGER STIFFLEMIRE ('60; HOF '05) lettered in football at Lee High and has enjoyed a long career in private and public education in two states, including a long tenure as principal of Prattville High School. He is now retired and educating his grandchildren—or vice versa.

JIM VICKREY ('60; HOF '94) was Lee Student Council President, award-winning Youth Legislature Speaker, and Senate leader. He was also SGA president at Auburn University, and he earned his Ph.D. degree in Rhetoric and Public Address from Florida State University. He served as president of the University of Montevallo (1977–88). After earning a J.D. from Jones School of Law in Montgomery, he practiced law and taught speech communication at Troy University (1991–2014). He retired in 2014, in part to work on this book.

ANNIE JOYCE (RIGGINS) WILLIAMS ('66) attended Alabama State University, married, and moved to Philadelphia. She worked 20 years for a publishing division of CBS, had two children, and graduated from LaSalle University. She also worked as a supervisor for US Healthcare/Aetna where she became a supervisor. Widowed, she still lives in Philadelphia.

Index

A
Adourian, Addie 66, 181, 196
Advertising Staff 116
AEA spring break 121
Akers, Mary 178, 193
Akin, Rex 125, 131
Alford, Randy 160
Allen, Richard 151
Allen, Rickey 143
Allison, Slugger 147
Alpine, Andy 149
Alred, Carl 149, 153, 156
Anders bookstore 29
Anderson, Charles 141
Anderson, Gerald 132, 135
Anderson, Jane 73
Andrews, Jimmy 160
Andrews, John 134
Andrews, Johnny 33, 35, 37, 129
Aplin, Andy 152
Arant, Mary Ann Pugh 196
Armstrong, Louis 12, 42, 127–161, 179, 195
Armstrong, Louis "Chip" 128, 156, 163
Arnold, Pookie 136
Arrington, William P. 24
Art Club 116
Atkison, Claudia R. 165, 195
Autrey, Frank 156, 197

B
Bach, Alice 37
Bach, Butch 156
Bagwell, Marjorie 66, 181, 193, 196
Baker, Phillip 150
Barbell Club 116
Barber, Danny 154
Barnhill, Don 150
Bartlett, Bessie 194
Bartlett, Haywood 12
Bass, Joe 152, 156

Beaird, Donnie 150, 152, 154, 155
Beaird, Ronnie 148, 150, 154
Bear Brothers Construction 4, 6
Bear, Fred 24
Beasley, David 142, 143
Beasley, George 197
Beasley, Johnny 145, 147, 150
Beasley, Terry 127
Beasley, Wayne 140, 145, 147
Beauty Ball 118
Beck, Joseph 171, 195
Bedsole, Bob 137
Bell, Elbert 156, 158
Bell, Jack 126, 131
Bell, Rodney 134, 136, 137, 140, 141
Berman, H. S., Jr. 4
Berry, James 142, 145
Berry, Russell 62, 63, 163, 180, 193, 195
Beshears, Buddy 158
Bessie Bartlett Student Loan Fund 194
Best, Sandra 196
Bice, Stafford 152, 156
Biology Club 111
Birkhead, Douglas 73
Bishop, Kenneth 159
Black, Freddie 131
Black, Jerry 143
Blackman, Larry 160
Blackshear, Helen x, 63, 180, 195
Blake, Louise Smith 197
Bobo, Thomas 55
Boland, Barbara 197
Bond, Dick 72
Bonnett, Billy 148, 152, 154, 155, 196
Booker T. Washington High School 59

Boone, Bubba 149, 153, 156, 160
Boone, Lee 10, 65, 196
Boone, Tommy 160
Borden, Thomas R. 72, 98, 171
Borders, J. C. 145, 149
Boswell, Walt 121
Bowman, Tad 72, 135, 137
Boyd, Bernard 151, 154, 158
Boyd, Bill 141, 143, 145
Bozeman, Howard 156, 158
Bozeman, James x, 17, 63, 163, 196
Bozeman, Wayne 135, 137
Brantley, Judy 72
Brassell, Lauryn x
Breedlove, Joanna 66
Brewer, Keith 158
Brice, Bonnie 72
Brock, Dalton 154
Brooks, Bob 197
Brooks, Dianne 197
Brophy, Charles 125, 129
Brophy, Earl 136
Brophy, Virginia 37
Brown, Danny 159
Brown, Ed, Jr. 149, 153, 156, 160
Bryan, Mike 152
Bryant, Jackie 130, 131, 134, 135
Buls, Bob 152
Burkett, Betty 105
Burleson, Rex 150, 151
Burson, Sarah 33
Byrd, Sim 148, 150, 151, 152, 153, 155, 158, 168, 197

C
Caine, Wayne 140
Cain, Jennie 196
Callaway, Jerry 135
Calloway, Jerry 132

Index

Campbell, Earl 145, 149, 150, 152
Cannon, David 71
Canterbury, Janice 37
Capitol Heights Junior High 10, 14, 18, 19, 22, 67, 105, 126, 129, 178
Capps, Glenn 150
Carlton, Annie Earle 9
Carlton, Timothy C. v, 4, 9–17, 35, 66, 67, 74, 104, 107, 128, 178, 191, 192–194, 195
Carr, Arlam, Jr. 48
Carr, Eva 196
Carr, Johnnie 56
Carr, Reese 134, 136, 138, 140, 141
Carter, Clinton 3, 9, 10, 12, 18, 25, 38, 46, 56, 62, 74, 99–103, 172, 191, 195, 197, 200
Cassaras, Donald 143
Castleberry, James M. (Mickey) 174, 196
Causey, Trey 132, 136
Cauthen, Fred 134
Cawthorne, Johnny 152, 155
Chafin, Jerry 134
Chafin, Jim ix, 18, 20, 63, 66, 124, 126, 128, 129, 131, 132, 134, 137, 138, 142, 143, 146, 148, 152, 155, 157, 159, 161, 177, 195
Chambliss, Linda Jemmott 195
Chemistry Club 111
Cherry, William 196
Choral Department 104–109
Choralees x, 105, 106, 107, 115
Christian, David 135
City of Montgomery 3, 40
Clark, Tony 151
Clary, Don 145, 149
Clements, Dollie 196
Cleveland, Bill 155
Cline, Jennings 73

Clower, Danny 156
Commercial Club 112
Cone, Chuck 160
Confederate symbolism ix, 20–23, 38–45, 83, 87, 89–91, 99–102, 136, 147, 172, 190
Conner, Wayne 138, 148
Cook, Mattie Bell 26, 67
Cooper, LaBaron 152, 154, 155
Cooper, Walter 129
Costen, Anne 180, 197
Couch, Charles 146
Courtney, Hudson 134, 136
Cox, Charles 64
Cox, Cliff 156
Crabb, Luther 72
Cramton Bowl 12, 28, 30, 31, 75, 83, 86, 95, 128, 133, 161
Crane, Joanna 163
Crane, Joanna Breedlove 195
Creel, David 149, 150
Crew, Doug 153
Crittenden, Julia 6
Crocker, Don 129, 131, 134
Crumpler, Frieda 106
Crysel, Charles 141, 146, 147
Crysel, Jimmy 132, 134, 136, 138, 141
Cumbus, Ben Joe 150, 154, 195
Cummins, Walter Clifton 24
Currington, Wade 142, 145, 147, 148, 196
Curry, Larry 131
Curtis, Joe 158

D

dances, dance styles 113–115, 117, 118
Danley, Mayme 67
Dannelly, Clarence M. 3, 36, 80
Darby, Leon 132, 134, 136, 137
Davenport, Ron 113
Davenport, Sammy 132
Davidson, Buddy 195

Davis, Donald 69, 119, 196
Day, Eunice 65, 180
Dean, Kitty 73
Deas, Charles Milton 197
Deen, James 151
DeJong Facilities Report 185, 187–189
Dendy, Mary Ellen 42
Dendy, Travis 179, 196
Denham, Betty Spruell Sandra 106
DePasquale, Raymond 143
DePasquale, Terry 156, 158
Dickey, Kenneth 135
Dillard, David 132, 135, 195
Dillard, Jimmy 151
Dillard, Tim 152, 154
Dinkins, Jim 104
Distributive Education Club 112
Diversified Occupation Club 112
Dobbins, Bill 134
Dodson, Mary Beth Shouse 196
Doe, Weldon 160
Donaldson, Tony 150, 154
Dorwart, Bonnie Brice 166, 195
Douglas, Lee 5
Dozier, George A. "Gus" 3, 80, 179, 197
Dramatics Club 111
Drinkard, Jerry 37
Dubose, Sara Ann 197
Dudley, Ellyn ix, 65, 105, 106–109, 195
Dunbar, John 131, 134
Duncan, M. T. 66
Dunn, Steve 156, 159
Dupree, Billy 134

E

Edwards, Chuck 197
Edwards, Henry 156, 159
Ellison, John 73
Ellis, Yale 77, 80
Engle, Ray 156, 159
Enslen, John 151, 155
Enslen, Robert G. 156, 158, 159, 197

Estes, Bert 138, 141, 145, 146
Evans, "Smokey" 126, 131, 132
Evans, Wayne 159

F

Farrell, Billy 152
fashions 120–121
Finney, Terrell ix
First United Methodist Church xii
Fisher, Tom 72
Flag Bearers 116
Flanagan, Pat 73
Fletcher, David 152, 156
Florey, Herb 142
Flournoy, Patsy 37
Ford, Leon 124, 127, 129, 131, 132, 134, 135, 136, 140, 143, 144, 145, 147, 151, 196
Forsythe, Jimmy 138, 141, 144
Foster, Cecil 146, 147, 149
Foster, Marcella 65, 67
Four Part Women's Music 115
Fox, Russ 156
Frandenburg, Jean 72
Frazierville 4
Frederick, Connie 158, 159, 197
French Club 111
Fuller, Frances 66
Future Homemakers of America 112
Future Teachers of America 115

G

Garner, Pat 125, 130, 149, 151, 153, 156, 157, 160, 197
Garnto, Don 160
Garrett Coliseum 32, 108
Garrett, Hank 147
Garrett, Richard 73, 196
Garrett, William S. 4
Gaston, Faye Barfoot 195
Generals Three ix, 105, 107

Gibbons, Frank 134, 136, 138
Gilley, Glen 140
Gilliland, Thomas 195
Girl Scout Troop 33 116
Girls' Ensemble 115
Givens, Dee-Dee 111
Glee Club 36, 105, 106, 107, 115
Glover, Danny 152
Godbold, Ronald 146, 196
Godley, Eudora Rodgers 196
Goode, Frances 37
Goodwin, Bill 135, 136
Goodwin, Charles 80, 165, 195
Goodwin, Foster 15, 179, 195
Goodwin, Sumter 179
Goolsby, Tom 181
Gordon, Dudley 136
Gowan, Thomas 147, 149, 151, 155, 197
Graydon, Wayne 129
Gray, Fred 48, 56
Green, Chris 196
Green, Derrell 151
Green, Keith 159
Gregory, Jan 33
Grimes, Ida 37
Grissette, Josephine 58, 67, 196
Groves, Ken 197
Grubbs, Milton 152, 156, 160
Gunn, Jimmy 152
Gunn, Joe 152
Gunn, "Skeeter" 131, 132
Guthrie, Dalton 33, 195
Guthrie, Greg 136, 137
Guy, Fred x, 17, 63, 195

H

Haigler, Larry 158
Hale, Kathleen 196
Hall, Elmore 65
Hall, Jim 72, 139, 142
Hall, Jimmy 135
Hall, Johnny 152
Hall, Leonard 138, 141, 146
Hall, Miles 147
Hall, Paul 152, 156

Hall, Randy 72, 142, 145
Hall, Richard 73
Hall, Wynona x
Hamilton, Billy 152, 154, 156
Hammett, George 91, 105
Hammett, Ken 105, 197
Hammett, Tom 104–109, 200
Hammett, Willie 105
Hamn, Ralph 159
hangouts and cruising 121
Hanna, Dickie 132, 134, 135
Hardin, Ed L. 179
Hardwich, Robin Bozeman 110, 200
Hardy, Warren 139, 143, 146
Harper, Bill 150, 195
Harp, Mary Ellen Dendy 196
Harris, Jimmy 155
Harrison, John 104
Hartley, Joan 73
Haynes, Johnny 104
Heaton, H. L. 33
Henderson, Bruce 73
Henderson, Lester 131, 134, 195
Henley, John 143
Herring, Buddy 147
Hicks, Diana 73
Hill, Lister 36
Hill, Richard 143
hobbies 122
Hobson, James L. 173
Hobson, Jimmy 141, 195
Hodge, Jo 67
Hodges, Phil 143, 149
Hoit, David 106
Hoit, Zane 72
Holleman, John 35
Holley, Billy 132, 135
Holley, Dorothy 67
Hollingshead, Tommy 157, 160
Holman, Donna 73
Home Economics Club 111
Hooks, Debbie Knight 110, 200

INDEX

Hopkins, Jay 150
Hopson, Carl 126, 127, 130, 131, 132, 133, 135
Hopson, Craig 136, 139
Horne, Donna xi
Horn, Walter 73, 197
Horton, Barbara Kenda 197
Howard, Peter 73, 74, 195, 200
Hudson, John 152, 156, 160
Huett, Judson 125, 132, 196
Huey, Frank E. 196
Huey, Martha 73
Huffstetter, Larry 154
Hufham, James W. 172, 197
Hufman, James 135
Hunt, Donald 130, 131, 132
Hust, Bill 148, 152
Hydrick, Bill 137, 141
Hydrick, Harry 135, 142
Hyland, Carol 197

I

Ingram, Harry 159
Inspiration Club 113
International Relations Club 117
Inzer, Virginia 72

J

Jack, Claudia Spence 197
Jackson, Eely 126, 129, 130
Jackson, Frank 197
Jackson, Sammye Norton 196
Jacobs, Grover 58, 196
James, Allen 135, 139
James, Alton 158
James, Donnie 137, 141
James, Earl 15, 42, 179, 195
Jenkins, Mickey 72
Jenkins, Rhonald 197
Johnson, Alex 147, 166, 195
Johnson, Carolyn 73
Johnson, Debbie Rice 196
Johnson, Frank xi
Johnson, Frank M., Jr. 48–54
Johnson, Freddie 151, 152, 154
Johnson, James 125, 131, 132

Johnson, Norma 197
Johnson, Rheta Grimsley ix, 200
Johnson, Sammy 159
Johnson, Sarah 63
Johnson, Steve 149, 152
Johnson, Wade 137, 158
Johnston, Freddie 148, 150
Jones, Charles 33
Jones, Charlie 132
Jones, Ed 124, 125, 197, 200
Jones, Tom 62, 67, 124, 125–161, 177, 178, 195
Jordan, John 145, 149
Jordan, LaFreeda 163
Jordan, Richard vi, 11, 126, 133, 191–194
Junior Classical League 112

K

Kamburis, Charles A. 37
Keldorph, Rusty 151
Kellum, Morris 159
Kelso, Kent 136
Kennedy, Annette 72
Kennedy, Bart 132, 134, 136, 137
Kennedy, Sam 197
Killian, John T. x
Kinard, Mike 160
King, Corrie 67, 180, 196
King, Karen 72
Kirby, T. A. 10
Kocial, Steve 72
Kransusch, Ken 129, 131
Kranzusch, Jim 151
Kuczmarski, Lloyd 147
Kwater, Jim 138, 148, 150, 152
Kwater, Larry 158
Kyser, Jerry 168, 196
Kyser, Kyle 168, 196

L

LaFollette, Lee 129
Lampkin, Keith 158
Lampkin, Leonard 72
Lancers Dance Band 92–94, 116
Lane, Norman 73
Lange, Jack 146

Lang, Jack 138
Lanier High School. *See* Sidney Lanier High School
Latin Club 35, 111
Lawson, Lola 180
Leader's Club x
leadership skills 118
Leap Week 118
Lee baseball 129, 131, 134, 137, 141, 146, 148, 151, 155, 159
Lee basketball 129, 131, 134, 136, 140, 144, 147, 151, 154, 158
Lee Concert Band 91–92
Lee Day 78, 110, 116, 117, 118
Lee, Durden 125, 196
Lee football 124–128, 130, 132, 135, 139, 143, 146, 150, 153, 157
Lee golf 149, 153, 156, 160
Lee High School. *See* Robert E. Lee High School
Lee Leaders Club 116
Lee, Pete 124, 132, 134, 139, 142, 143, 145, 152, 156, 157, 159, 177, 181, 196
Lee, Robert E. 5, 20, 43–45, 190
    statue and portraits 24, 38–42, 176
Lee track 130, 132, 135, 139, 142, 145, 148, 152, 156, 159
Lee weightlifting 137, 151
Lee wrestling 132
Lenoir, Burton 143
Letter Club 11
Leverette, Virginia 179
Lewis, JoAnn 37
Library Club 111
Lide, Jerry 72
Lide, Rod 19
Lindley, Doug 197
Lindsey, Annie Laurie 22, 63, 182, 196
Lions Club 12, 15, 89, 169
Little, Cliff 125, 129, 130, 131

Little, Marie 111
Livings, John 131, 134, 170, 197
Long, John M. 63, 67, 78–98, 100, 104, 195
Long, Mary Lynn Adams 80, 89
Loveless Academic Magnet Program 184
Lucas, Dan Warren 167, 197
Lydon, Terry 73

M

Maddox, Floyd 152, 155, 159
Mallory, Jimmy 150
Maloney, Kathleen 73
Mann, Gaddis 150
Mardi Gras 118
Marlar, Marian 164, 180, 195
Marshall, Donald Alan 166, 196
Marshall, Mitchell 158
Marshall, Warren 154
Marsh, Marion 72, 73
Martin, Dale 72
Martin, Louisa 73
Marvin, Albert 152
Mason, Mike 152, 156
Mayo, Larry 153, 156, 160
McArdle, Joseph 42
McCain, George 104, 197
McClinton, Buddy 159
McCracken, Spence 159
McCurdy, Jean 67
McDavid, Joel xii
McDevitt, Ray 169, 197
McDonald, Joe 126, 130, 131
McFarland, Robert 152
McGilberry, Joseph 195
McGilberry, Nell Rushton 11, 63, 197
McGuff, Shirley 72
McKee, Walter 88
McKnight, Mickey 134
McLendon, Mac 149, 153, 156
McNair, Bill 125, 129, 167, 197

McNeil, Ken 156
McNight, Mickey 131, 137
McWhorter, Horace 72
McWhorter, Tommy 73
Meadows, Benny 126, 130
Meads, Larry 154
Mears, Delmus 154
Medley, Guy 62, 67, 80
Meier, David 73
Melton, Gene 160
Melton, Jimmy 163
Metts, Toby 150
Meyers, Martha Crystal 196
Middleton, Jimmy 158
Miller, Craig 130, 132
Miller, Kay Kennedy 169, 195
Milligan, Ronnie 150, 151
Mills, Earl 125, 126
Mills, George 160
Milton, Gary 156, 158
Mitchell, Wayne 148, 152, 155, 195
Mize, Rennie 143, 146, 147, 196
Montgomery Advertiser 16, 36, 40
Montgomery County Board of Education 3–6, 9, 16, 33, 42, 46–55, 125, 179, 184, 186, 187, 189, 190, 199
Montgomery Improvement Association 56
Moore, Bobby 132
Moore, Jane 73
Moore, John 131, 132, 134, 136, 137
Moreland, Jerry 136
Morelock, Ed 130, 131, 132
Morgan, Mike 152, 154
Morgan, Patricia 72
Morris, Larry 141, 144, 145, 146, 171, 195
Moseley, Alec 138
Moseley, Alex 136
Muse, Carol 72
Music Appreciation Club 115
Myers, Martha 73
Myrick, David 147

Myrick, Ricky 151, 155

N

NAACP 46, 58
Nagel, Eddie 156, 160
National Merit Scholarship Program 71
Nation, Robert 156
Neel, Buster 159
Neese, Hulon 136
Nelson, Joseph, Jr. 197
Newman, Mickey 125
Newton, Gary 159
Nichols, Gladys 58, 62, 65, 75, 100, 180, 193, 195
Nixon, E. D. 46, 55
Nobles, Wayne 149
Nolan, Janet 172, 196
Norred, Sarah Graham 195
Norton, Phil 143
Norwood, Thomas 72
Numismatists Club 116

O

Ohme, Paul 132, 134, 136, 196
Oliver, Warren 147
Overstreet, James 160

P

Pace, Jack 73
Palmer, Carol 105
Palmer, Glenn Fair 197
Palmer, Kerry 77, 201
Panhorst, Kathy 37
Parent-Teacher Association 33
Parham, James 129, 131, 134
Park Crossing High School 187
Parker, Henry A. 35
Parker, Randy 158
Parker, Raymond 125
Parker, Rob 105
Parker, Roy 196
Parma, Marie Little 19, 197
Parrish, Tommy 153
Paterson Field 32
Peek, Brad 152
Peters, George 67, 127
Pettus, David 73
Phillips, Don 138, 141

Physics Club 111
Pickett, John 13, 28
Piel, Richard 142
Piel, Shorty 147
Pierce, Laurence 72
Pierce, Laurens 122, 197
Pierce, Leroy 41, 197
Pilgreen, Ernie 143
Pitts, Bonnie 72
Poole, Arlon 156
Poole, Pete 150
popular entertainment 119–120
Porter, Billy 143
Posey, Neal 125, 127
Powell, Judy 73
Price, Carolyn 72
Price, J. L. 62, 67
Pricket, Charles 135
Pride of Dixie Marching Band 76, 82–91, 97, 99, 116
Priester, Dory 159
Priester, Joel 159
Priester, Louis 157, 158, 159
Pritchard, Charles 132
Program Service Club 116
Pruett, Guerry 154
Pugh, Mary Ann 37
Putnam, Dorothea 67

R

Radio Club 116
Ramsey, John David 138, 146
Reeder, Paul 37
Reeves, Andy 142, 143
Reeves, Otis 154, 197
Renfroe, Kyle 126, 179, 192, 195
Rentz, Frank 141, 146
Reynolds, Ed 196
Rhone, Larry 150, 151
Rich, Elizabeth 73
Riggins, Joyce. *See* Williams, Annie Joyce (Riggins)
Riggins, Willie, Jr. 54, 55–57, 201
Riggs, Anacile 67
Riggsby, Dutchie 195
Ritter, Robert 139, 142, 143, 145, 196

Robert E. Lee High School
and athletics 30, 37, 57, 117, 124–161
and desegregation 22, 23, 28, 38, 46–61, 98, 102
and discipline 29
and quality of education 57, 71–76, 94, 109, 162, 182
and religion xii, 27, 42, 66, 70, 76, 113, 127, 178
and technology 25
clubs and activities of 66–67, 106–107, 110–123
dedication of 35
enrollment of 4, 7
expansions of 6–7, 82, 178, 185
faculty and staff of 7, 25, 28, 62–67, 178–181
future of 184–190
Hall of Fame of 41, 64, 162–175, 176
lunchroom of 26
music program of 35, 37, 41, 76, 77–109
naming of 4, 5, 190
origins of 3–6
student backgrounds of 68–70
traditions of 18–24, 30–32, 33, 78, 95, 113, 116, 182
Roberts, Howard 143
Roberts, Jim 73
Robertson, Paul, Sr. 179, 197
Robinson, Alice (Bach) 19, 22
Robinson, Randy 148
Rogers, Rick 149
Rowell, Clinton 196
Rowell, Johnny 154
Roy, Billy 135
Rucker, Neal 131, 132
Rudd, Frank 156, 160
Rushton, Danny 132
Rushton, Nell 72
Rutland, Jack 11

S

Saari, Carolyn 71
Salter, Kitty 37
Sanders, Julia 54, 55, 57, 59–61, 201
Sanders, Larry 130, 132, 135
Sanders, Peter 73
Sandlin, Bobby 131
Sandusky, Sue 65
Scabbard, The x, 20–21, 57, 70, 71–73, 111, 113, 118
Scott, Travis 197
Scott, Wayne 72
Scribblettes 116
Seabury, Glen 73, 155
Sellers, Don 129, 132, 134
Sellers, Wayne 146
Senior Girls' Club 113
Sertoma Club 4
Sessions, Don 154
Sessions, Faye 67
Sexton, James 136
Sharits, Diane 72
Shell, Barbara 71
Shell, Julia 195
Shepherd, Bill 129
Sherlock Smith and Adams 4
Sherman, Tom 154
Shine, Glenn 150
Sidney Lanier High School 3, 5, 16, 31, 33, 48, 77, 124, 130, 162
Sims, Bobby 156
Sims, Jimmy 145
Sims, Robert 37
Skipper, Darrel 156
Skipper, Darrell 196
Skipworth, Lena Frances Dean 197
Small, Ann 106
Smith, Bayne 73
Smith, Buddy 135, 139
Smith, Charles 128, 143, 145
Smith, David 146, 148
Smith, Doug 145, 148
Smith, John 135, 137, 160
Smith, "Juddy" 131, 132, 134
Smith, Mary 67
Smith, Terry 72

Smithwick, Eddie 159
Smyth, Louise 14, 26, 28, 67, 178, 195
Snaider, Richard 72
Southernaires Dance Band 92–94, 116, 165
Sowell, Nancy 73
Spanish Club 111
Spear, Ann McLean 197
Spear, Jim 196
Spears, Henry 54
Spears, Louise 54
Speight, Charlotte 67
Spencer, Ed 125, 129, 130
Spencer, Jackie 125, 129, 130, 131
Starr, Becky Sullivan 164, 195
Stars and Bars, The x, 14, 21, 22, 23, 24, 33, 35, 63, 65, 85, 112, 113, 119, 120, 121, 127, 161, 165
Steeley, Mike 73
Steiner, Robert E., Jr. 24
Stephens, Suzie 105
Stevenson, Joel 154, 155, 156, 157
Stifflemire, Roger 43, 161, 196, 201
Stout, Randy 151
Strange, Todd 186
Stroud, David 135
Suggs, Fred 196
Sullivan, Grant 197
Sullivan, Joe 73
Surles, Louis 134
Sutliff, Richard 73
Sutliff, Sarah xi
Switzer, John B. 174, 195

T

Tarica, Albert I. 170, 196
Tatum, Charles 125, 130, 132
Tatum, Eugene 152
Tatum, Glenn 156, 160
Tatum, Greg 152, 158
Tatum, John 148, 152, 154, 156, 167, 196
Tatum, Ware 141, 143, 144
Taylor, Carolyn 72

Teague, Mike 160
teas 113, 120
Thames, Billy 197
Thespian Club 111
Thompson, Ann 67
Thompson, Dane 37
Thompson, George 163
Thompson, Mary 162, 163, 196
Thompson, Phil 135
Thornton, Ben 152, 155
Thrash, Ed "Rudy" 197
Thrash, Jane McSwain 197
Thurman, Danny 155
Thurman, David 152
Traylor, Tommy 159
Tucker, Don 134, 136, 197
Tuley, Jim 148, 152
Tuley, Mike 72, 179, 196
Tulley, Jim 154, 155
Turner, Billy M. 196
Turner, Thomas 195
Turnipseed, James 158
Twirlers 116
Twirp Week 113

U

Urk, Melvin 35

V

Vann, Larry 137
Vaughn, Harry 148, 152, 155
Vick, Errol 135
Vickrey, James F. xii, 41, 64, 122, 162, 163, 176, 184–190, 195, 201
Vinson, Bill 131

W

Waites, Angeline 71
Waites, Dickie 150, 151
Walker, Don 196
Walker, Mac 153
Warren, Walter 146, 147, 150
Warr, James 141, 195
Warr, James W. 173
Washington and Lee University 24, 44, 45
Waters, Sue 37
Watts, Ted 197
Weaver, Woody 144, 196

Weinard, Rock 153
Welch, Davey 160
Welch, David 156
Weldon, Margaret 62
Wells, Lance 148, 152, 154, 156, 197
Whiteside, Worth 72
Wienard, Rock 149
Wiggins, Barbara 163
Wilkes, Billy 132, 136
Williams, Annie Joyce (Riggins) 54, 57, 58–59, 201
Williams, Billy 126, 131, 134
Williams, Kent 72
Willis, Betty 72
Wills, Jerry 155, 158, 159, 197
Wilson, Alan 131, 134
Wilson, Billy 151
Windsor, Jerry 137, 151
Wingard, Joe 196
Wingard, Sam H., Sr. 196
Wohlford, Eddie 106
Wood, Ben 135, 136, 139, 140
Woodham, P. L. 64, 195
Wood, Ken 154, 158
Wood, Mason 139
Woodmen of the World 33
Woolard, Fred 197
Wyatt, Bobby 37
Wyatt, Donna 37

Y

Yancey Park 84
Yeck, Gary 150
YMCA x, 76, 113, 115, 116, 118, 137, 166
Young, Earl 132, 135
Young, Laura Childree 195
Young, Ricky 149, 152, 156

Z

Zorich, David 145, 148